DOS RIOS MEMORIES

The story of Alonzo Hartman –
Pioneer cattleman and
one of the first settlers
on Colorado's Western Slope

by

Judy Buffington Sammons

Raspberry Creek Books, Ltd.

**RASPBERRY
CREEK**

BOOKS

DOS RIOS MEMORIES

Cover design by
Kym O'Connell-Todd

Photos on Pages 1, 11, 25 and 77
By Larry K. Meredith

Other books by
JUDY BUFFINGTON SAMMONS

Graves of the Gunnison Country: Dunsmith Publishing House, Ltd., LLC, 2011

By an Act of Congress – A Biography of Lewis Easterly, co-authored with Robert Easterly, 2011

Keepin' the Peace – Early-day Justice on Colorado's Western Slope: Western Reflections Publishing, 2010

Riding, Roping, and Roses – Colorado's Women Ranchers: Western Reflections Publishing, 2006

Tall Grass and Good Cattle – A Century of Ranching in the Gunnison Country: Western State Colorado University Foundation Inc., 2003 (3rd edition)

Acknowledgments

Many thanks to Larry Meredith of Raspberry Creek Books, Ltd., for turning my stack of papers and pictures into a real book. Help with research was provided by several people – their loan of materials or expertise lends to the book a meaningful authority. Many of Alonzo Hartman's original writings as well as the "turn of the century" Hartman family photographs were generously lent for review or copy by Western State Colorado University's Dr. Duane Vandenbusche – the book would not be complete without them.

Thanks to Hugh Pressler for sharing his collection of several years' worth of newspaper clippings on the Hartman family. Thanks to writing colleague Bob Easterly for researching the photograph collection and the files on the old Los Pinos Indian Agency at the Denver Public Library.

A most enjoyable day was spent with guide Gib Kysar hiking to the old Hartman cabin in Hartman Gulch for pictures. Thanks to the Gunnison Pioneer Museum for allowing access to their Hartman files and photographs. Joyce Hartman of Montrose, a distant relative of the Alonzo Hartman branch of the family, provided valuable family information as well as family photographs. Thanks to the Montrose County Museum for information on the Hartman brothers' Paradox Valley project.

I appreciate the Denver Public Library's allowance of use of photographs of the old Los Pinos Agency – one taken by William Henry Jackson himself. JoAnne Williams dug through many Ancestry.com files, assisting me with census information, for which I am grateful. The staff at the

Gunnison County Courthouse -- County Clerk's office – was most helpful in assisting me with property searches.

Thanks to Western State Colorado University's library staff for assistance with archival material as well as letting me frequently camp out in their Helen Jensen Western History Room. Thanks to rancher Lee Spann for letting me "pick his brain" on more than one occasion. Attorneys Rufus Wilderson and Dick Bratton are appreciated for their contribution of information and expertise on water issues. The excellent photograph of the San Luis Valley was provided by photographer Allan Ivy.

I very much appreciate historian Duane Vandenbusche's help with details of the story and his comments about it. Thanks also to Lee Spann and Kathleen Curry for reading the book for accuracy and commenting on it.

Last but not least...thanks, as always, to my photographer friend, Walt Barron, for his contributions to four previous books as well as the excellent pictures taken for this one – pictures bringing the old Hartman mansion back to life.

Table of Contents

Colorado

The Gunnison Country

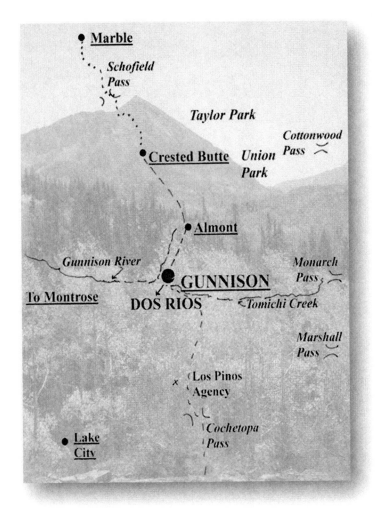

(The author's reference to "the Gunnison Country" – a local term – describes a large area comprised of all the land drained by the Gunnison River and its tributaries, which includes some land outside the county's boundaries. Its borders are roughly the Elk Mountains to the north, the old Denver and Rio Grande railroad station of Cimarron to the west, Lake City to the south and Monarch Pass to the east.)

DOS RIOS MEMORIES

For that old Nebraska pioneer . . . my mother,

Betty Hill Buffington

Introduction

I n 1872 a young Alonzo Hartman – handsome, square-jawed and rugged, but of a kindly nature and smart – came across a gentle crossing of the Continental Divide, Cochetopa Pass, and rode into history as the first cattleman in what would soon become known as the Gunnison Country.

Riding with Hartman was Otto Mears, later to become Western Colorado's famous road builder. Their destination was the Los Pinos Indian Agency located in southwestern Colorado at the foot of Cochetopa Pass, about 30 miles southeast of present-day Gunnison. As they crossed the Divide, the Ute agency was not yet in sight; it was only a quiet empty valley they saw, but they agreed that it was "quite the country." Before and above them were big handsome skies, gentle hills covered with silvery sage, and off in the distance, superb high peaks reaching into the blue. Alonzo Hartman would fall in love with this country and would put his roots down deep here. His trade would be agriculture – cattle ranching.

Three decades later Hartman would be firmly established in the nearby Gunnison Country, and his Dos Rios mansion, from where he managed 2,000 head of cattle, would have become a landmark in the region. He would in time operate one of the most extensive ranching and cattle

Alonzo Hartman, about 1930
Courtesy Gunnison Pioneer Museum

operations on the Western Slope of Colorado. Alonzo Hartman was one of the first pioneers to the Gunnison Country and had come when the area was wholly uncivilized. A.W. Bowen described in his 1905 book, *Progressive Men of Colorado*, Hartman's arrival to the area: "He boldly strode into the wilderness when what is now Gunnison County was a part of Lake County and an Indian reservation with no white man within fifty miles of where he 'stuck his stake' and there challenging fate, determined to meet her on almost equal terms."

Shortly after Hartman's arrival at the Los Pinos agency with Otto Mears, he was appointed as chief caretaker of the government cattle that were grazed some thirty miles away, near the present site of Gunnison, where at the time, there was no sign of civilization for miles in any direction. The town of Gunnison, however, would soon be born at this location and Hartman would be instrumental in the birth and development of it, so much so that many considered him, along with another founder, Sylvester Richardson, a "father of the Gunnison Country."

Other than his own brief memoir written late in his life and titled simply, *"My Life,"* no biography has been written of him. This book will be the first. Two years of extensive research went into the writing of it, not the least of which was examining Alonzo's own collection of writings which recorded his memories of early-day Gunnison history, compiled when he was an older man and retired in California. This material, inherited by Alonzo's son Bruce, was donated to Dr. Duane Vandenbusche of Western State Colorado University's History Department and was lent to me for review. The material is original - written in Hartman's own hand. A few of these stories were published in Gunnison's 1930's era newspapers, but most have been unseen, to date.

I also read whatever books or material I could find on the history of early-day Gunnison. I especially enjoyed re-reading works by my old high school English teacher, the late Betty Wallace. Her *History with the Hide Off* and her Master's Thesis, *Six Beans in the Wheel* are wonderfully written works chronicling Gunnison's early history. I studied the files on the Hartman family housed in Gunnison's Pioneer Museum as well as their collection of early-day Gunnison newspapers. A great pleasure was taken in visiting Hartman's three original residences – all survive – his historic "Hartman Castle," his stone house on Wisconsin Street, and his very remote cow camp cabin in Hartman Gulch, a large ravine that branches off to the right near the top of Lost Canyon Road. Also surviving is Hartman's original post office, now sitting on the grounds of Gunnison's Pioneer Museum. With the help of photographer Walt Barron, excellent pictures of these residences resulted. Priceless historic "turn of the century" photographs were borrowed and copied from Dr. Duane Vandenbusche's Hartman collection and Savage Library's archives at WSCU, from Gunnison's Pioneer Museum, and from the Denver Public Library (these with the help of writing colleague, Bob Easterly).

A part of the story of Alonzo's life remains somewhat ambiguous. A reason for this is that Annie and Alonzo Hartman had no grandchildren. There are no living descendants to interview who could shed light on some of the more or less blank spots in the family history, especially the later years. Also, there are somewhat divergent renditions of more than a few of the incidents in his life and by now, with the passing of the years, it is impossible to ascertain which of those renditions is most truthful. Therefore, the following biography is not the final say on his life, but is representative of the historical research performed.

Hartman's mother, Mary Boone Hartman, claimed to be a descendant of Daniel Boone. She had filled her children's heads early on with the exploits of their famous ancestor who had been an American icon for a century before Hartman came to the Gunnison Country. Like his famous ancestor, Alonzo had a very remarkable and interesting life, one which was representative of a fascinating time in the growth, expansion and early settlement of the West. This important historical period when the Western Slope of Colorado was entirely unsettled was the backdrop of Hartman's life. Fitting into it, he would in time be remembered as a "top hand" as a cowboy, a friend to the Utes, an entrepreneur, originator of a new town, and finally as a respected and prosperous rancher.

When the Utes were moved from the agency on the Cochetopa in 1875 to the Uncompahgre Agency near the present day town of Montrose, Alonzo assisted in the move, trailing the government cattle to Montrose. A few years later, in August, 1881, he would sadly watch as his friends, the Utes, were driven out of Western Colorado, leaving their beloved old summer hunting grounds in the Gunnison Country and departing from the Uncompahgre Reservation near Montrose, from where they were herded on a 350 mile march to a reservation in Utah.

From then on Hartman's story is very much the story of the development of ranching in the Gunnison Country, he being among the first in the area. Hartman's early cowboying days at the Los Pinos Agency's cow camp near Gunnison had served to whet his appetite for the cattle business. At the same time Hartman genuinely mourned the passing of the Utes. He also welcomed those who would take their place - the growing number of settlers and ranchers coming into the country, and soon declared about them and himself, "The cattleman, till about 1914, was king of the Gunnison Country – the rivers and hills were his."

After the departure of the Utes from Los Pinos in 1875, the cabins and corrals of the cow camp were given to Hartman by the government. Beginning his life of entrepreneurship, he and a co-worker, Jim Kelly, decided to capitalize on their location near the confluence of two rivers, the Tomichi and the Gunnison, and freighted in some supplies and set up a store. Then they brought more cattle in from the San Luis Valley. Hartman immediately took up the cow camp land as a homestead, calling it the Dos Rios Ranch. Where two rivers meet is always a good location; it would be near the center of the activity that was about to start up in the Gunnison Country due to growing acclaim for its fabulous silver deposits. A mining boom was quickly developing.

Hartman, seeing that growth and changes were coming, quickly began capitalizing on his assets to advance his ranching business. He sold property to the new railroad, the Denver and Rio Grande, as access and used the proceeds to invest in more land and buy more beef. He branched into various other businesses and occupations from time to time, all the while taking a lead role in building up the new town of Gunnison. But he remained essentially a rancher and was generally considered the local authority in the livestock business and in 1894 a committee of his fellow ranchers elected him as the first president of the fledgling cattlemen's association.

Alonzo's rough beginnings in the crude cow camp lodgings may have made a lasting impression on him. Perhaps he got his fill of drafty, uncivilized log cabins with primitive fireplaces and dirt floors; mice and loneliness being constant companions. He later married and built for his wife Annie, the "Hartman Castle," by far the fanciest of the early ranch houses in the area. The castle at Dos Rios boasted a tower with ascending arched stained glass windows, a white oak staircase, parquet floors and fancy wood filigree everywhere.

The Hartman's stay at the "castle" lasted some two decades. Here he and Annie raised a family of three children, all of whom eventually left the area and scattered to the winds. Perhaps one of Hartman's biggest disappointments in life was that his son Bruce was apparently not interested in continuing on with the management of the Hartman empire. Although there is uncertainty about his motives now - a century later- it appears that Hartman, disappointed by his son's unwillingness to carry on with the ranching business at Dos Rios, and faced with his own advancing age, eventually, and against Annie's wishes, sold the Dos Rios. He then invested, along with two of his brothers, in a water project in the extreme northwestern part of Montrose County in the Paradox Valley. This water scheme eventually failed and nearly proved to be his undoing. After the fiasco of this Paradox water project, his resources greatly depleted, Alonzo and Annie spent much of their time visiting at the homes of one child or another, eventually residing with their daughter Leah in Mojave, California until their deaths.

Hartman lived to the ripe old age of 90, his early pioneering trials and hardships not shortening his years. Tributes from friends and admirers at Alonzo's death painted a picture of a brave and adventuresome man - driven and successful, but at the same time kind and generous - very much a family man – about everything a man should be. Hartman was a genuine, bonafide cowboy of the Old West, too. A friend remembered of him: ". . . he was at much at home in the saddle on a long day's ride over cattle range, as the average citizen today feels in his parlor rocking chair . . ." It was of these kinds of grand days that Alonzo wrote near the end of his life. Living far from his much loved Gunnison ranch and home, Alonzo spent his last years occupying his time writing of the early days – the exciting days – the Indian days – the pioneering days in the Gunnison Country.

Dos Rios Memories

Part 1

Go West Young Man, Go West

Horace Greeley

Alonzo Hartman was born on September 3, 1850 on a farm near Iowa City, Iowa. The town of his birth was fairly well established by the time he arrived in the world, and had a population of around a thousand. Iowa City was located in eastern central Iowa Territory and for a short while served as the territory's capitol. The pretty little town was located on bluffs above the Iowa River. Some of the early-day buildings, constructed about the time of Alonzo's birth in the mid-1800s, still survive. Iowa's first territorial governor's home still stands as does the "Old Capital" building. Once serving as the seat of government for the territory, the home has survived since 1840, and is now a museum.

Thomas Hartman, Alonzo's Father
(Date unknown)
Hartman Family Photo

Alonzo's mother Mary, right, on the steps of the Hartman Castle at age 70. On the left is Annie's mother Mary Haigler, with their granddaughter Leah in the center. Photo taken in 1904.

Bruce Hartman photo

Alonzo's parents had both come to Iowa City shortly after the town came into being. Here they met and eventually married in 1848 when Mary Boone was seventeen and Thomas Hartman was thirty. Alonzo's father, originally from Canada, had taken up a homestead near Iowa City, finding the country a rich agricultural mecca which allowed him in time to become a prosperous farmer. Alonzo's mother, who claimed to be a descendant of Daniel Boone, had originally come west to Iowa with her parents from Pennsylvania. During the eight years that Alonzo, second child of the family, was to live in Iowa City, the family grew to include six children, two not surviving infancy or childhood. Four boys would survive, however, and a fifth boy would be born in Kansas.

Four of Alonzo's brothers with his father Thomas standing center. Standing at left, Edward. Flavious (Joe) is at right. Seated are Charles, left, and Samuel. Date unknown.

Hartman Family photo

Alonzo was born during a very significant period of American history – the great wave of western expansion began shortly before his birth with the California gold rush. The "49ers" – thousands of them - rushed to the far West. At around that same time, the Treaty of Guadalupe Hildago, had brought an official end to the Mexican-American War. Now 500,000 square miles of former Mexican territory, including all or parts of what would later become several western states, including a part of

Colorado, were eventually to become new territory – new homes - for the young Alonzo and his four brothers.

Alonzo's first eight years of life in Iowa City, before the Hartmans joined with so many others moving westward, were typical for a child of that age. The older Hartman boys, during this time, received spotty and limited educations in the one-room country schools of the day. At home they were responsible at an early age with assisting with the farm chores. According to Hartman's memoirs, written much later in his life, the family was a happy one. He always spoke of both his father and mother with warmth and respect. He had special fond memories of the family sitting around the fire – all ears – listening to his mother's stories about their ancestor, Daniel Boone. Hartman wrote: *"My mother was very proud of her ancestor . . . and she spent many long winter evenings telling us tales of his bravery, his strength, his kindness, and his unselfishness . . . I suppose that is where we all got our love of adventuring and pioneering."*

In 1858, when Alonzo was eight years old, the Hartman family moved to Hiawatha, Kansas. There is nothing on record to indicate why this move was made. What brought them to Kansas from a reportedly prosperous farm in Iowa is now unknown. Also very little is known about the family's five-year stay in Hiawatha. Kansas had a rural economy and it can be assumed that Thomas Hartman continued his farming occupation there. Kansas was a considerably "wilder" place than the one they left, however, and not far removed from Indian Territory. It had become open for settlement in the 1850s and soon towns sprang up catering to the cattle trade.

Hiawatha was located in the fertile rolling hills of northeast Kansas; it had been founded in 1857, only a year before the Hartmans came. In typical western style, its main street was called Oregon Street after the Oregon Trail and side streets were named for Indian tribes.

Alonzo reported in his memoirs that things did not go well for his father in Hiawatha, Kansas and that while their farm yielded abundant crops . . . so did everyone else's and there was no market for his father's produce. He also reported, *"For many weary months my mother, four brothers, and I had seen the emigrants streaming westward, in a slow, but never-ending line past our little farm . . . in 1860 father got discouraged with farming and decided to join the immigrants heading west."*

After Thomas Hartman's departure, the family, headed now by Mary, was left alone to fend for themselves and to wait for word from the absent father, not knowing where he was or even when, or if, he would return. Many months went by before a letter was finally received. He had become a late member of the "59ers – Pikes Peak or Bust" gold rush. Hartman had bought a "good claim," he said, in the mountains in a place known as California Gulch. He said he wasn't worried about the family he had been forced to leave behind, as so many others had - he knew they could grow plenty of food on the farm to eat. Even so, he promised to send money. That badly needed money was to be sent east to Kansas with a cousin. The cousin never arrived and neither did the money.

The family survived, however, and during a Kansas drought, when little food could be grown, they lived mostly on a diet of rabbits for a number of months - in later life, Alonzo would refuse to eat them. The nearly desperate family hung on now until the next letter arrived containing the long awaited news that Thomas was coming back to retrieve the family and as soon as the roads opened in the spring, was taking them back with him to what was now Colorado Territory and the newly established town of Denver.

The Hartman family sold their farm, provisioned themselves, and joined the many caravans headed west. Alonzo later reported that they followed the overland trail via the Platte River. Many times they were delayed by great herds of buffalo and on one occasion their route was blocked by a buffalo migration for half a day.

Their journey over the westward trails in a "prairie schooner" or covered wagon pulled by an oxen or mule team, was typical of such journeys at the time. Food was plain, consisting of flour or corn meal, bacon, sugar, coffee, salt, rice or beans, and whatever game could be brought in along the way. Cooking was done over a campfire at night, with anything from wood to buffalo chips to sagebrush for fuel. The journey was fraught with danger; cholera was rampant and many died from it along the way and Indian attacks were always a possibility. The young Hartman brothers did not seem to see anything negative about the trip, however. Alonzo tells the story of this journey through the eyes of the exited thirteen year old boy he was at the time, "*So in the spring of '63 at last we had taken our place among those steadily rolling wagons – rolling west with the sun over the long, lush prairie grasses toward the dim mountain peaks which reared gleaming white turrets high above the flat prairie floor. During our trip we passed great herds of buffalo and*

17

had been thrilled at the sight of graceful antelopes leaping off across the prairies. We met some Indians, but they were friendly; they had not yet begun to molest wagon trains, but a year or so later emigrants were to meet with much trouble from warlike tribes of plains Indians."

Although the plan for the family upon arrival to their destination was to head for the mountains where Thomas Hartman's placer claims were located and work the claims until winter set in, they decided to first camp close to the town of Denver for a couple of weeks. Newly established Denver, which was building up fast, but which in outer areas looked like little more than a mining camp, was described by Alonzo thus, *"At first sight it looked like a huge sprawling city of tents. The streets were filled with strangers like ourselves, and there seemed to be no end to the stream of covered wagons, coming and going. It was all very different and exciting to us boys."*

And so after crossing the Great Plains to Colorado Territory from their more established towns in Iowa and Kansas, and finding only a city of tents (some of them tepees) and roughly built log cabins, the family then moved on to a primitive mining camp near their father's placer claims in the mountains. The rough camp conditions must have been a trial for Mary Hartman, made even more so by what Alonzo later reported were Indian raids that resulted in some of their neighbors losing their lives.

The older boys, after having assisted their father in the warmer months, came back to Denver during the winter months to try and attend school. The next winter in 1864, Alonzo, with his brother Charlie, now young teenagers, decided to stay in Denver year around and not go to the mines. Their plan was to work somewhere for board and room so they could attend school. They eventually found a place – a boarding house – where they could work for a place to sleep in the unfinished attic.

Alonzo's life as a teenager seemed to consist of a hodge-podge of jobs alternating with off and on attendance at school and off and on residence at his parents' various homes (camps or cabins.) At about age fifteen, Alonzo again worked in mines, whether his father's or others, and at whatever other jobs he could find around Denver and in Golden and Central City. For a time, he attended school at Denver Seminary, the first high school in Denver, although he never completed his education there. (The last grade he officially completed was the 6th grade earlier in Kansas.) Between the ages of fifteen and seventeen, Alonzo again assisted his father who was now in the cattle business. At seventeen, he struck out on his own and worked for a range cattle outfit, assumedly located near Denver, buying and selling cattle. Sometime in between these various engagements, according to Alonzo's son Bruce, in a 1971 correspondence, "Thomas Hartman became close to the pioneers who, with Buffalo Bill Cody, left North Platte, Nebraska when the railroad came west. Alonzo and his father helped supply meat for the railroad workmen: buffalo, antelope, and rabbits for quite a distance." Bruce Hartman also reported that, "all the while this was going on, the mother and the younger boys lived in a cottonwood log cabin located in Denver." Alonzo said of this period in his life, "*I guess I was like most boys, always trying to think what I should do for a living when I should have to get out in the world and rustle for myself, I began to think of the future when I should have been attending school . . . but the country was new and schools were scarce . . . "*

Eventually Thomas Hartman sold his mine and bought a ranch in Littleton, Colorado. By then Alonzo and his brothers were older and were having thoughts of getting out on their own and seeking greener pastures further west. In 1870 at the age of twenty Alonzo moved to the San Luis Valley, located southwest of Denver. This valley, historically inhabited by the Ute Indians, had earlier (in the 1850s) seen some Hispanic settlement but only after military forts had been established for protection against the hostile tribes. The Utes had been entirely removed from the San Luis Valley by treaty in 1868, and thus it was open for further settlement by the time Alonzo arrived two years later.

San Luis Valley much as Hartman saw it in 1870.
Allan Ivy Photo

"It was quite the valley," Alonzo reported, after first seeing the San Luis. What he saw was one of the largest mountain desert valleys in the world. The valley reaches an altitude of over 7,000 feet and is roughly 100 miles long and 60 miles wide. Bordered by the Sangre de Cristo Mountain range and Mt. Blanca to the east and the rugged San Juans to the west, it is a place of long vistas and immense skies. This great quiet valley had been home to several Indian tribes, and to the early Spanish priests. It had seen the passing by of explorers such as Juan Maria Antonio Rivera, Zebulon Pike and John Fremont. Nearby were two of the West's most notable forts – Bent's Fort near present day La Junta and Fort Garland near present day Alamosa. The forts' histories were probably first-hand knowledge to Alonzo – it's possible that he even supplied beef to one or both them during his two years as a young cattleman in the San Luis Valley. Fort Garland had only recently been commanded by the legendary Kit Carson. Alonzo undoubtedly heard firsthand the tales of the famous scout and Indian fighter's stay there.

A.W. Bowen, who interviewed Alonzo Hartman for his 1905 book *Progressive Men of Colorado*, states: "In 1870 he (Alonzo) moved into the San Luis Valley with a herd of cattle and started a cattle and ranching business of his own." It is possible that Alonzo brought his herd of cattle down the Front Range from the Denver area to the Walsenburg area, then over La Veta Pass into the San Luis Valley. Another scenario is that he did not buy the cattle until he reached the Arkansas Valley and then, after the purchase, moved the herd into the valley. Cattle grazing opportunities had expanded here after the removal of the Utes and these new opportunities were what brought many new settlers like Alonzo into the San Luis Valley at this time.

Little is known about his first independent foray into the cattle business – Alonzo does not speak of it at all in his memoirs or relay whether it was a success or a failure. Therefore it is not known if he leased land or grazed cattle on free range somewhere in the valley . . . he apparently did not own land of his own. Whatever his experiences were – good or bad -- for the two years he spent in the San Luis Valley, it is known with certainty that he soon decided to move on to the almost entirely wild and empty Western Slope and the Gunnison Country.

At the end of the Civil War and up to the time when Hartman arrived there, the Western Slope of Colorado lay undisturbed by the nation's westward movement. There were no railroads, no roads, no towns -- only Indian trails and Ute camps. However, it was not completely unknown to the white man. It had earlier been visited by the Spanish explorers, the mountain men, and by military and private exploration searching for good routes for the transcontinental railroad. As early as 1853 Captain John Gunnison's Army of Topographical Engineers had passed through regions of the Western Slope and by 1860 a few small mining parties had been in and around the Gunnison Country, mostly in the summer months. These were all transient visitors, however, and when Alonzo arrived from the San Luis Valley to the Western Slope it was entirely Ute country.

As more and more white men had entered their territory in Colorado, the Utes found themselves pushed further and further into western Colorado. As a result, in 1869 they had been placed on reservations, under the auspices of "agencies" – the White River Agency for the Northern Utes and the Los Pinos Agency for the southern tribes. Alonzo's older brother Charles had accompanied the first group of Utes to arrive at the Los Pinos reservation and had helped establish them there. Perhaps his brother's description of the new country on the Western Slope and the new Los Pinos Agency intrigued Hartman. If he could find a way to legitimately intrude into what was strictly Ute territory, he could easily reach it from the San Luis Valley where he was located, via Cochetopa Pass. This pass was an easy, all-weather gate to the Western Slope. It had historically been used by the Utes when following the buffalo and other game. But recently it had become a supply road, built by Otto Mears in 1869 to transport supplies to the newly established reservation.

In time it also would serve as a passageway to brand new country for a very adventuresome, young Alonzo Hartman. As to the outlook of this new territory, according to author A.W. Bowan, "The region was remote, uninhabited by settlers and devoid of roads . . . all who were there had to 'rough it' in heroic style. The life was strenuous enough to satisfy the most adventurous and the outlook sufficiently unpromising to deter all but the most determined."

Dos Rios Memories

Part II

The New Eldorado

The West that Hartman had known as a boy changed as he grew into manhood. The huge, vast, wild, and unknown area west of the Missouri was slowly approaching some degree of civilization. The nation's first transcontinental railroad was completed in 1869 meaning travelers could ride from New York to San Francisco in an unheard-of eight days. Peace treaties had ended some of the Indian conflicts and the West's Indian threats, while not entirely gone, were winding down.

Indians would, however, continue to play a large role in Alonzo's life for some time to come. The Ute Indians – the tribe that Alonzo would have association with for many years – initially became known to him upon his family's arrival to the Denver area. A common site on the plains east of Denver at that time was of Ute tepees. In fact, several years earlier, an agency had been established near Denver for them. The Utes hunted in the mountains nearby and also hunted buffalo on the plains. After coming back from these forays they would rendezvous in the city of Denver. To Alonzo, they became a familiar sight. In his memoirs, he speaks of becoming acquainted with some of the Denver Utes and also with what he called the "government men" at the agency. One of his various jobs, in fact, was helping with the cattle on the reservation. After this experience, he always maintained sympathy and admiration for what he called *"these wild children of nature."*

Coming next, would be the Ute's gradual progression from the eastern to the western side of the Rockies a route that was essentially followed by Hartman. Alonzo states in his memoirs that the Utes were moved from the Denver reservation, as more and more settlement took place there, to a place where they would have bigger hunting grounds and be, as he said, *"far from ever-reaching civilization . . . the Gunnison country was chosen as the site of a new agency as it was then a wild, unsettled region – no roads or bases of supplies to attract settlers or prospectors, or so the government thought."*

The various Ute tribes had traditionally roamed across most of Colorado and parts of other nearby western states as well, hunting and raiding. They had been known by various names: Yutas, Utahs, and Blue Sky People and were divided into seven different bands, located in different areas. The area where Alonzo and the Tabaquache or (Uncompahgre) band would eventually reside – the Gunnison Valley and land nearby - had already seen Ute occupation as early as 1650 after the acquisition of the horse from the Spanish. The Utes traditionally occupied the Gunnison Country's mountain valleys only for summer hunting and moved to warmer climates during the winter months.

Chief Ouray, eventually to be well known by Hartman, had been designated in an 1863 U.S. treaty as "head of all the Ute bands." This treaty was an attempt to move the Utes away from the eastern slope and the San Luis Valley to new locations further west. Most of the

27

various bands of Utes never recognized this treaty and it had to be reaffirmed in 1868, about the time Hartman began pioneering in the San Luis Valley.

A Ute teepee at the Los Pinos Agency with a brush wickiup nearby. A photo by William Henry Jackson (1874).
Denver Public Library # 1X-30650

A Ute camp at Los Pinos with a herd of goats and a brush shelter. Taken between 1868 and 1875.
Denver Public Library #1WHJ-1396

The treaty of 1868 allocated nearly one-third of Colorado, the western third, to the Utes. This allocation was described as a reservation, the eastern boundary of which was the 107th meridian, only a few miles west of the future sites of Gunnison and Crested Butte, and extending west to the Utah line. The Utes, ousted now from the San Luis Valley, were moved to the Los Pinos Agency on the Cochetopa which became their home and headquarters. This it remained for several years until unwelcomed mining activity by white interlopers to the Ute reservation escalated in the San Juan Mountains. The conflicts between the Utes and the persistent miners, insistent on encroaching on the Ute's land, led to the Brunot Treaty of 1873 which cut the San Juan area out of the reservation and moved the location of the agency.

After his experience with the Utes in Denver, Alonzo Hartman came into the Indian picture again shortly after they were moved to the Cochetopa area. After his arrival in the San Luis Valley in 1870, his ranching endeavors had evidently not been overly successful because by 1872 he was earning his living by working in the little trading town of Saguache at Otto Mears' general store. There he met numerous people coming and going, including many Utes who still traded there. Stories abounded concerning the new reservation just across the Divide. Hartman's curiosity was peaked and he reported, *"I had been hearing these stories going the rounds until I was anxious to learn all I could about this 'new Eldorado' just around the corner.* At the store, Alonzo had a chance to meet the current agent at the Los Pinos Agency, General Charles Adams, who suggested that if Hartman wanted to see the "new Eldorado" he should accompany Otto Mears on one of his trips to supply the agency with goods and then stay on for a while.

A Ute delegation with Otto Mears standing at left.
Date unknown.

Museum of Western Colorado

Alonzo's employer, Otto Mears was later to gain prominence as one of Colorado's most progressive and successful pioneers. He had come to the San Luis Valley in 1866 and bought government land near the present-day town of Saguache. Mears was instrumental in starting that town, which was platted in 1867. He soon established a "general store" there and was planting wheat on his farm. In addition he started a career of road building by developing roads around the Saguache area and nearby. He also operated pack trains from Denver to Saguache via

La Veta Pass and freighted in goods from Denver and from as far away as Santa Fe. Mears was a Russian immigrant who had come to America young and uneducated. Early on he became aware of the opportunities that existed in the West, and began to take advantage of them. In various parts of Colorado he started several enterprises, including building toll roads and railroads. He would become involved in politics and have a successful political career in the state, even though he was sometimes accused of using "dirty politics." Mears claimed to be a friend to the Utes and acted as an interpreter, being somewhat fluent in their language. But at the same time, he was later one who was instrumental in their being removed from Colorado.

Mears was in the early stages of his remarkable career when Alonzo became acquainted with him and was hired to work in his Saguache store. Mears had recently, in 1869, transformed the route over the Cochetopa Pass from an Indian trail to an extremely rough and primitive wagon road. The new road covered 55 miles, over which Mears trailed 100 head of beef per month to supply the Utes with meat. He was also transporting vast amounts of flour, beans, coffee, sugar, oats, and hay. Government supplies that came to Saguache from Fort Garland, including blankets, tents and clothes were also lurched and bumped over this perilous road to the agency by Mears.

Alonzo finally got his chance to visit the agency. On August 1, 1872, at 7:00 a.m., he and Mears (Alonzo riding what he described as a *"good horse")* started out on the 55-mile journey to the Los Pinos Agency. The trip was made in ten hours without a stop. At the summit of 10,000-foot Cochetopa Pass Alonzo began to see the prospects of the new country below. It was remote and far removed from any signs of civilization, a country of gentle rolling hills, lofty mountains, beautiful open parks, and steep canyon walls. Meeting at the confluence of Cochetopa and Los Pinos creeks there was a broad valley and a natural park, the location of the Los Pinos Agency – the "new Eldorado."

What Alonzo saw upon his arrival at the agency can best be described as it was by an earlier visitor, R.B. Townshend, in his book *A Tenderfoot in Colorado.* "The site of the proposed agency was a lovely natural park on the Rio de Los Pinos, a branch of the Cochetopa. The first frosts had painted yellow and scarlet the quaken aspen and dwarf oaks . . . every hill top was crowned with tall red-stemmed columns of the pines, while the rich bunch grass covered the slopes. The cone shaped tepees of the Utes stood in clusters . . . boys were coming up from the creeks with strings of trout, and the bucks were riding in from the hills with venison and elk meat hanging from their saddles."

The first thing that came to Alonzo's attention as he and Mears neared the agency were the great numbers of lodges scattered over the sagebrush plains for almost a square mile. Alonzo estimated that there were from 3,000 to 4,000 Indians camped here at an elevation of about 9,000 feet. Alonzo observed the agency itself which had been built in 1869 and by now was comprised of several administrative buildings, a school, and a seldom used saw mill. An adobe house had been built for Ouray and his wife Chipeta in a corner of the square. All in all there were a dozen or so buildings placed in a 200-foot quadrangle. Alonzo reported that most of the houses appeared to have been built of logs, then plastered with mud and whitewashed.

Ouray's old home at the Los Pinos Agency as it appeared in the 1930s. The walls were boarded up to protect the crumbling adobe structure.

J. B. Lloyd photo

The original Los Pinos cellar as photographed in 2012.

Author's collection

The day of their arrival, Alonzo and Mears were greeted by Chief Ouray and his wife Chipeta who both impressed Hartman greatly and with whom a lasting friendship was begun. Chief Ouray had been born in New Mexico, the son of a Jicarilla Apache father and a Tabeguache Ute mother. By the time he was an adult, Ouray could speak the Spanish, English, Apache, and Ute languages. At the age of eighteen he moved to what would become Colorado and became a member of the Tabeguache Ute tribe, eventually becoming its chief. As chief he sought peace between the conflicting interests of the Native Americans and the whites. For this he was considered a coward among the more militant sub-chiefs of the Utes, many of whom were also jealous of his position. According to Hartman, Ouray loved his horses and guns and . . . *"talked good English if he was speaking to one whom he knew he could trust, but he conversed with most white men in Spanish. He and I became fast friends and I often talked with him in English."* Alonzo found Chipeta to be a typically shy and submissive Ute woman. She was tall and slender-considered a beauty by admirers – and Ouray seemed devoted to her and very proud of her.

Buckskin Charlie, at one time thought to have been designated Chief of the Southern Utes (a claim later proved false). At 6'2" he was known for his physical presence and his courage.

Photo – Museum of Western Colorado

A Ute delegation showing Chief Ouray and his wife Chipeta seated at the right. Standing behind them is General Charles Adams. The other three are identified as Ignatio, The Hon. Carl Schurz (of Missouri), and Woretsig. Date is unknown.

Photo courtesy Museum of Western Colorado

Alonzo stayed three days at the agency, taking in the sights and getting to know the Indians and the agency in general. He got acquainted with several chiefs - Ouray, Sapinero (also called Sapavanero,) and one he called Curicata. Alonzo noted that the Indians spent most of their time horse racing, an occupation at which they were experts. He also noted that they had very good horses. Horses seemed to be a major concern of everyone, white and Indian alike, and Alonzo was soon involved up to his neck in this pursuit. Chief Ouray, whom Alonzo had just recently met, offered to let Alonzo try to ride a horse that was described as a *"fine looker, but not thoroughly broken."* In fact, even the best rider at the agency had been unable to stay on him. Alonzo accepted the challenge . . . *"I put my saddle on the outlaw – then the crowd began to gather (all the agency folks and about 200 Indians) to see the visiting tenderfoot ride the wild mustang . . . I hopped on and the fun began . . . they all seemed disappointed because I didn't role off in the dirt all broken and bruised and crippled for life."* After successfully riding the horse, a confident Alonzo now became like an old friend to the Indians and they crowded around, slapping him on the back and asking him how he had tamed this horse that no one else could ride. Alonzo explained to the impressed crowd that he had spent much of his life on western cattle ranches and had hunted buffalo and chased wild horses across the plains, and so had some experience.

In his memoirs, Hartman, during his first three-day stay at the agency, made many interesting observations about the Utes and their practices. Ute warriors, he claimed, whose jobs had only recently been fighting battles - mostly a thing of the past - were mainly occupied now by hunting game and bringing it to camp and caring for their horses. Alonzo was impressed with the Ute camps and said, *". . . one who has never visited a Ute Indian Camp should see how neat and comfortable they are in their tepee tents with a fire in the center and smoke curling out through a little ring at the top . . ."* He also claimed *"Most of the Indians understood little or no English nor did they seem interested in learning any. . . The Indians spent summer and fall hunting and preparing the meat for winter. They were careful to kill only as much as they*
36

needed. The agency supplied them with rifles and ammunition so they did not have to depend on bows and arrows."

Alonzo observed with interest that the Ute's tepees were made of both heavy canvas, supplied by the government, and also elk hides. The Utes were furnished with blankets, which Alonzo noted they wore around their shoulders or hung from their arms. The bucks were issued suits, but wore only the coats and vests and ripped up the pants for leggings. Squaws, as Alonzo called them, were furnished cloth for garments, and dresses were made by simply cutting a hole in cloth for the head – a belt was fastened around the middle. The Indian women covered leather moccasins and garments with beads in intricate and beautiful designs. Papooses were carried in cradle boards on the mother's back. Hartman made interesting observations about the division of labor claiming *"the squaws . . . true to tradition, did most of the hardest work when moving camp, jerking meat, and tanning hides. The bucks concerned themselves largely with hunting. Their manner of eating varied little from that of their wild state. They ate principally roast meat, game, bread and coffee . . . the Indians did not grow vegetables or fruits except for wild varieties . . . "*

As Alonzo undoubtedly recognized, prior to reservation days the Utes had been a hunting tribe acclaimed for their skilled horsemanship. The game they hunted provided them adequately with food, clothing, and shelter and they had no need to take handouts from the government. Some of their buffalo hunting skills lived on, however, and as Alonzo was soon to witness, slaughter of beef for the Indian's use was accomplished as a kind of organized raid on the beef – one indeed resembling a buffalo hunt. The animals were corralled, and mounted Utes with rifles and revolvers in hand waited until the gate was opened and the frantic cattle rushed to escape. At a later date Ernest Ingersoll, while traveling with photographer William Henry Jackson and Ferdinand V. Hayden with the U.S. Geological & Geographical Survey, and at the agency in 1874, saw the same beef killing event and gave this description: *"The steers, indeed, were wilder than buffaloes, and dashed away at high speed, surrounded by a little crowd of shrieking Indians, whose fringes and bright blankets flashing in the sunlight with rapid movements of the horses, made a very lively picture. It lasted only a few moments, however, before the rifles and revolvers began to be heard, and the agonized cattle dropped in their tracks, yielding up their hides almost sooner than their souls."* Ingersoll also reported about his visit to the agency, *"The tribe possessed some six thousand horses – and about six hundred thousand dogs."*

William Henry Jackson, the famous photographer who was along on the Hayden survey at the same time Ingersoll was, made a valiant effort to photograph the Utes at Los Pinos. After his group arrived at the agency, Jackson was able to photograph Ouray, Chipeta, and Chief Piah, whom Jackson described as "the most photogenic." The next day all the rest of the Utes refused to have their pictures taken because one of their chiefs, Shavano, said it would make them sick and they would die. Jackson attempted to take several pictures after this but he was physically stopped by the Indians. What images he was able to capture are an invaluable record of life at Los Pinos much as it was when first seen by Alonzo Hartman.

After their three-day stay at the Los Pinos Agency, Mears and Hartman returned to Saguache. Mears seemed to have been impressed with his companion on the trip and after their stay at the agency, hired Hartman to help him repair and improve the Cochetopa Pass road in preparation for delivering supplies to the agency before winter set in. Laying the groundwork for this, the two made a trip to New Mexico where they bought 10,000 pounds of beans and 75,000 pounds of potatoes. The potatoes, once delivered to the agency, were stored in the cellar. The potatoes went to waste, however, because the Utes, who were unfamiliar with them, refused to eat them.

Alonzo retired from his duties at the general store and became Mears' "right hand man," going with him and helping fill contracts with the government for Los Pinos. This job ended when all contracts were completed on November 1, 1872. Alonzo was then asked by Agency Agent Adams to stay on at the agency and take the position of post storekeeper. Adams was likely as impressed with the industrious young Hartman as Mears had been, and soon – in the dead of winter - reassigned him to a more responsible post – that of keeper of the government cattle at the agency's cow camp located near the present site of Gunnison, some 30 miles away.

* * *

On September 13, 1873, the Los Pinos Agency was the site of the signing of the Brunot Treaty. Felix Brunot, a wealthy eastern steel executive, along with some three hundred Utes headed by Chief Ouray, watched the ink dry on parchment that gave some four million of the sixteen million acres of the Ute Reservation back to the United

States. This parcel contained the fabulously rich San Juan mineral lands. The Brunot Treaty, along with the agency's location at a very high elevation that was too cold for Utes habitation in the winter months, was responsible for the closing of the Los Pinos Indian Reservation on the Cochetopa. The Utes were moved in 1875 to a location at a lower elevation – the newly established Uncompahgre Agency (sometimes known as Los Pinos II) located 12 miles south of present day Montrose, Co. In 1880 a bill known as the "Ute Bill," designating the exclusion of the Utes from Western Colorado, was signed by the president. In 1881, the Los Pinos or Uncompahgre Agency Utes, were moved to a reservation in Utah located next to the Uintah Reservation. The new agency's name was changed to "Ouray Agency." These two agencies were consolidated in 1886.

On August 24, 1880, Chief Ouray died while visiting the Southern Ute Reservation at Ignacio, not living long enough to witness his people's tragic removal from western Colorado. Chipeta, often described as an "Indian princess," because of her beauty and bearing, died forty-four years later in 1924 at the age of 81 on the Utah Reservation. She was nearly blind and living in poverty.

The Los Pinos Agency was sold in the early 1880s to rancher John Thompson McDonough – all the buildings and the adjacent land included. The main agency building was used for a house by the McDonough family. Chief Ouray's house was used as a blacksmith shop. In time all the original buildings of the agency were torn down. The McDonough family maintained ownership of the "Old Agency Ranch" for eighty-two years. It remains a ranch today, a beautiful, well-kept ranch - now in new hands. All that is left from the Indian days is the original cellar – now converted into a wine cellar - but which was once seen or used by the likes of William Henry Jackson, Otto Mears, Alonzo Hartman, Chief Ouray, and even the notorious Alferd Packer.

A Ute delegation in front of an agency building at Los Pinos around 1872.

Colorado Historical Society

John McDonough at the old Los Pinos Agency shortly after he purchased it in 1881.

Author's Collection

Dos Rios Memories

Part III

The Cowboys
And the
Cow Camp

An earlier agent at the Los Pinos Agency, Adam Trask, who was replaced by General Charles Adams in July of 1872, had reported, shortly after he came to the agency, that the stock were in very poor condition. He said the beef were "lean and miserable," the sheep "thin and worthless." The sheep and cattle at the agency were short on feed and had no shelter, which he thought was cruel. To improve this situation, he established a "cattle camp," as he called it, near the present site of Gunnison, which, although located nearly 30 miles from the agency, was situated where there was exceptionally fine grazing land. A possible contributing factor for the poor grazing conditions at the agency was the presence of thousands of Indian ponies. If, as Ernest Ingersall reported earlier, there were some 6,000 of the tribe's horses grazing near the agency, grass was probably quickly depleted. It was this new cow camp, established only a year earlier, that Alonzo was to report to now.

Following Agent Adams' directions, Alonzo traveled alongside Cochetopa Creek and Tomichi Creek to reach the cow camp. It was bitterly cold and desolately quiet when he came within sight of the primitive log cabins of the camp. He had just crossed through the snow covered sagebrush flats at the foot of Tenderfoot Mountain and had surveyed his situation. That coming winter more snow would fall, in some areas to depths of four or five feet. There were no roads to the nearest civilization (which were Ute Indian camps) for many miles in any direction. He would be in charge of keeping what he reported to be 3,000 head of cattle and 2,000 sheep alive through a severe winter with thousands of Ute Indians dependent on this source of food for their survival. He was twenty-two years old.

The day that young Hartman arrived at the camp was Christmas Day, 1872. He showed up at the cabin in a blinding snow storm, soaking wet, and riding a government mule. The cow camp's little crew greeted him, according to Alonzo, and *"soon had a good blaze in the fireplace and some hot coffee, and I was soon OK."* Alonzo, who was now to be in charge of the cow camp, would be working with fellow employees James Kelly, chief aide, and Sidney Jocknick, cow puncher. (Some accounts also list a Herman Leuders.) Later the town of Gunnison would sit near where they camped, but for now they were the only inhabitants in the Gunnison Valley. These three would pass the winter in a rough log cabin that was the only dwelling in the area.

The first year the cow camp existed, it had been manned by government employees James Kelly and Joseph White. In fact, they built the cabin at the cow camp. It was situated just west of the union of the Tomichi and Gunnison rivers. Although Kelly had been put in charge of the camp when the first stock was brought in a year earlier, (640 cows and 1160 sheep,) his position, by orders from General Adams, was to be reassigned to Hartman. (The reason for this is unknown.) The main job of the crew was to move cattle and sheep from one grazing area to another to find the best grass available. During the winter the livestock were located for the most part along the Gunnison and Tomichi rivers, where they could root through the snow to find dry grass. Water holes had to be chopped open every day in the frozen rivers along the banks. In the summer months the crew would move the herds to new grass – sometimes as far away as Taylor Park, some 30 miles to the northeast.

Hartman, in his memoirs, described his first winter at the cow camp: *"We spent the winter there without seeing anyone for over three months."* Hartman, Kelly, and Jocknick cared for the hundreds of cattle and sheep in deep snow, having to move the animals constantly to the places where it was possible to find grass – a seeming impossible task. However, Hartman claimed to have *"never lost a single one"* that winter.

Hartman's stay at the cow camp would last from December 25, 1872 until the fall of 1875. For these three years he shared bachelors quarters with the other men in the little cabin located in the middle of nowhere with, for the most part, no other civilization in sight. Most of the time they worked. It was a constant job to care for the livestock. Chopping wood to burn in the fireplace and stove was an unending task. Provisions were probably occasionally packed in from the agency. Food was plentiful but undoubtedly must have been a tedious fare of trout, elk, and beef. Alonzo described the Gunnison Country as *"abounding in game – deer, elk, mountain sheep, mountain lion, bear, wild cat, and lynx . . . streams teeming with beaver and mink."* The crew had unbelievable fishing opportunities on the Gunnison and Tomichi rivers; trout fishing at this time was a fisherman's dream. Alonzo described their method of catching and cooking fish: *"first put the fat in the skillet and put it on the fire, then grab the fishing tackle and catch a fish and have it ready for frying by the time the fat was hot. One was a plenty as these fish would weigh from 1-2 pounds . . . and trout taken from these ice cold waters and cooked soon are the finest eating in the land."*

For entertainment the crew participated in elk hunts. One is vividly described in some length by Sidney Jocknick in his book, *Early Days on the Western Slope of Colorado.* Jocknick claimed that the crew's usual Sunday occupation was hunting coyotes.

While these young men probably relished most aspects of their experience, such as the total independence - the freedom - the adventure, it must have also been a confining, lonely life at times, one accompanied by the constant presence of danger. There was no medical assistance, if needed, and help for any other calamity was miles away. The sometimes 40 degrees below zero weather must have been a shock to those used to milder climates. However, both Hartman and Jocknick, when in later years writing their memoirs, offered not a single complaint about their years at the cow camp.

Much of the essence of what it would take in the future to be a success in the cattle business in the raw new Gunnison Country, comes through in Hartman's memoirs. Complaint about the difficulty encountered, is entirely lacking. Acceptance of the elements and the necessity of keeping livestock alive by whatever means is also clear. But another of the early cow camp residents, Sidney Jocknick, who was at the camp off and on during the same three years as Alonzo (possibly hired because he spoke some of the Ute language) described these early cowboying experiences a little less enthusiastically. . . *"Here, nothing could be prophesied, except that it was a life of hard knocks, as well as a life of toil and sacrifices . . ."*

Hartman, who went on to become a successful and prosperous rancher, whereas Jocknick did not, relished the challenges of the cow camp from the very beginning. He wrote the following account of his first encounters with the milk cows and Longhorns who had earlier strayed from the Indian agency and the Cochetopa area. This wild herd had not only survived, but had increased to several hundred. *"I found that some of the cows were still so gentle that I could ride up close to them. The steers were fine large fellows but so wild it took a pretty swift horse to keep up with them. But I had been furnished with some fine cow horses and several men to help so we succeeded in corralling some of them and driving them back to the agency. Several took to the high timber, and we never did catch them."*(It has long been suspected that many of these escapees were "borrowed" a few years later, helping several pioneer ranchers get their start.)

Occasionally there were visitors to the cow camp. In July of 1873, the Parsons Expedition, which came to the area with intentions of exploring the Gunnison Country, arrived at the Los Pinos Agency with thirty men and eight teams. Either Chief Ouray or the agent gave them permission to continue on into Ute Indian territory. From the agency they traveled on to the cow camp and camped there. They relayed their intentions to eventually settle in the valley to the surprised cow camp crew. The three bachelors must have been pleased at the welcome news of having, at last, some neighbors.

Sidney Jocknick tells in his *Early Days on the Western Slope of Colorado* of another group that arrived that same year. In December, he relays, a starving group of prospectors from Chief Ouray's winter camp in Delta (the Utes did not usually stay at Los Pinos in the winter) stumbled into the cow camp. Enquiries of the group revealed that they had been directed to the cow camp by Chief Ouray (against his better judgment) and had parted from six other men whose group was headed by the infamous Alferd Packer. Packer's outfit should have reached the cow camp a week behind the first group but they had instead taken a "cut off" which led them to the Lake City area and the horrendous tale of murder and cannibalism that would follow. *(See note about Packer at the end of this chapter.)* Meanwhile the party of five that had made it to the cow camp were provisioned by the crew and recuperated for several weeks at the cow camp before they moved on as spring approached.

Other than brief visits to the Los Pinos Agency, Hartman was almost always at the cow camp attending to duties. But by the summer of 1875 those duties were coming to an end. Following the signing of the Brunot Treaty, mentioned earlier, the Utes were scheduled to be moved to the new Uncompahgre Agency near present day Montrose. The Ute cattle herd was to be moved too. Subsequently, one of the Western Slope's very first cattle drives, at least one of any significance, took place that summer. A herd of 800 cattle were moved from the Gunnison area, from as far away as Taylor Park, to a location by the Uncompahgre River, some 75 miles away. It would prove to be an undertaking of extreme difficulty. Hartman, Kelly and Jocknick were expected to trail the Ute's live beef supply through the exceedingly rough terrain between the cow camp and the new agency. Sidney Jocknick writes of this trip in detail in his book, describing a trip that was *"plagued by difficulty from the very beginning."* The following is a summary of his account.

The crew from the cow camp and a few greenhorn assistants – all novices at trail drives - after rounding up the herd, started out on the journey. Foremost among their problems was the decision to transport the provisions of the trip aboard a "prairie schooner" fully loaded and requiring three yoke of cattle to pull it. The overloaded wagon soon proved to be a hindrance which was solved by throwing all unneeded items overboard. Progress was slow, not only because of the cumbersome schooner, but the little calves – unaccustomed to travel – soon became footsore and fell behind, their mothers staying back with them. Ten miles a day was average progress.

As cattle and riders reached exhaustion, grass became short and water nearly nonexistent. The result was a restless, thirsty and unmanageable herd. The outfit moved miserably through an alkali dust cloud and conditions soon became ripe for a stampede. The wretched thirst of the cowboys apparently overrode the thoughts of an impending catastrophe and it was decided by the crew that emergency measures must be taken. They determined that the situation could best be dealt with by breaking into a keg of "good old Gukenheimer" carried aboard the schooner.

Alonzo, acting as "trail boss," seemed to feel that his position required of him that he act as bartender for this occasion and he proceeded serving liberal drinks. Drinking of the straight liquor on empty stomachs and with no water to wash it down inspired a round of melodramatic toasts by the crew. Perhaps they shouldn't have let down their guard, for the cattle had in the meantime smelled water and were making a wild stampede for the Uncompahgre River.

All eventually reached their destination safely, Jocknick summing up the trip with this comment, "*when the trail wasn't up a mountain it went down into a bog . . . slow, but sure mileage and distinctively western, and taken as a whole, it was anything but the snap that such trips are usually cracked up to be.*"

Moving the cattle herd had been one thing – moving the agency equipment, the Utes and their possessions, was another. According to Hartman's memoirs . . . "*It was no little job to move all the agency stuff over the 75 miles of mountains and deep canyons. No wagons had ever passed this way - only Indian trails. The Indians have ponies and pack their stuff all on these ponies* (on travois) *then each Indian has also a pony to ride and these ponies are tough and hardy and can stand the hard knocks. They are never fed anything just turned loose to hunt their living.*" The Indians took their time moving, stopping to hunt and fish along the way.

After the Los Pinos Utes had been moved to the Montrose area, taking the cattle with them, Hartman and the other two men were out of jobs. But things had slowly started to change in the Gunnison Country and Hartman, seeing new opportunities, stayed on. The previous winter of 74-75 had seen the settlement grow from the cow camp crew to some twenty other people scattered here and there throughout the valley, including Sylvester Richardson who had come earlier with the Parsons expedition in 1873, and was one of the few of that original party who had stayed on.

Sylvester Richardson, variously known as a geologist, druggist, assayer, teacher, lawyer and historian, among other things, upon first seeing the Gunnison Country became greatly excited about its agricultural possibilities. Richardson returned to Denver with the Parsons Expedition – his soul burning to return to the Gunnison valley. He organized a "colony" – a group of pioneering souls who would accompany him with the intent of settling that isolated region west of the Divide. He came back in 1874, with his colony, hoping to develop the country for some kind of agriculture - ranching or farming. For the next four years a small number of them struggled on, making limited progress.

Even though most of the excitement in the country centered on nearby Lake City's gold strikes, and even though there were only a very few settlers in the Gunnison Valley in 1875 when the cow camp ceased to exist, there must have been enough civilization stirring to indicate promise to Hartman, for he and Jim Kelly stayed on. He described this significant step in his life in his memoirs:

"I was given the cabins and corrals (of the cow camp) *as it would not have paid to move them. Jim and I freighted in supplies and set up a little store in one of the cabins. We brought some cattle from San Luis valley and grazed them there. We had to get supplies from Pueblo and Colorado Springs, a hard, tedious*

journey over almost impossible roads and trails in summer and completely impossible most winters so we had to use a lot of foresight in buying. However, our store more than paid us, for people began to arrive in large numbers because of the gold discovered at Lake City . . . Jim and I moved our cabins near Gunnison, and in 1875 I took up a homestead on the Gunnison River. The Tomichi joined the Gunnison there; so I called my ranch Dos Rios . . . Here we were in the center of activities."

Alonzo Hartman's Dos Rios Ranch in 1876 showing the Post Office and the cabin built in 1870. From Betty Wallace's "History with the Hide Off."
Betty Wallace photo, Grant Houston Collection

Top left: Hartman's original Post Office restored and sitting on the grounds of Gunnison's Pioneer Museum.
Walt Barron Photo

Below: the Post office as it appeared in 1930. It had earlier been the gathering place for many Utes and early-day pioneers.
J. B. Lloyd Photo

For a time, after he opened his store, Hartman had a quite profitable business of trading with the Utes who were allowed to travel from the Montrose Agency to trade and hunt in the Gunnison Country in the warmer months. With them he exchanged buckskins, bearskins and other types of fur for coffee, sugar, cartridges, matches, and beads. Nearly fifty Utes would crowd into the store dressed in their finest clothes – buckskins covered with bead work. The Indians arrived at the store on their ponies, camped nearby, and stayed a few days. Alonzo reported that after Chief Ouray died, Chipeta, who had gone to live with her brother Sapinero, came every summer for a long time to visit him. *"Sometimes Sapinero came with her and we would have long tales by the fire. He was a dear friend. Sapinero was now the big chief and last I saw of him was about 81 just when the*

54

*government was moving them to 'Uinty' (Uintah Reservation
in Utah) . . . when it was settled they were to go the old chief
Sapinero saddled his best horse and rode to Gunnison sixty miles
to have a little visit with me and say a last good bye . . . he stayed
two days and he sure was a good faithful friend. . . I gave him
1000 cartridges so he need never have to buy any more as long as
he lived."*

In 1875, along with filing for a homestead, Alonzo
also filed, with Water District 59, the Gunnison Country's
first claim to a water right. The claim was on the Gunnison
River, filed May 10, 1875. He then constructed a ditch
which was fed from the river. Other very early filers (from
1875 to 1877) were John Outcalt, the Vidal brothers,
Tingleys, Teachouts, and Purriers. There were 16 filings by
the very earliest pioneers before 1879 when the town was
incorporated. The length of Alonzo's ditch was one mile,
the depth 2.5 feet, and the grade 30 (fall of 30 feet per mile.)
The amount of water it would carry would irrigate 200
acres. Shortly after this first claim, Alonzo added 360 more
acres to his holdings which he brought under irrigation the
next year - 1876. At the time it was estimated that 1 cubic
foot of water would irrigate 40 acres and therefore Alonzo
was allocated 14 cubic feet in a later ruling. According to a
1903 map connected to the water filing, Alonzo's ditch ran
through his own property and ended up near the Lewis
Hotel in the town of Gunnison (Later renamed La Veta
Hotel).

As Gunnison began to build up Alonzo realized the
necessity of supplying the town with water and offered to
build and maintain eight miles of ditches to make some of
the water diverted from the Gunnison River available to

the town. His offer was accepted and soon water was coursing down both sides of the new streets in the new town.

Colorado became a state in 1876, although there were so few people in the Gunnison area there wasn't much of a celebration. Mail was now coming into the area, though, from Lake City. The same year that Colorado became a state Alonzo was appointed postmaster at the Gunnison settlement – one of the original cow camp cabins served now as the post office: *"I had the post office and had to carry the mail myself, or we didn't have any. We went once a week to Powderhorn, 'White Earth' was the name then . . ."* With the establishment of the new post office the mail route had changed and now came to Powderhorn via Saguache. Alonzo retrieved the mail by horseback and on snow shoes, traveling the twenty-eight some miles from his new post office to Powderhorn and back one or two times a week. Alonzo's rigorous mail trips stopped in 1880 when the Barlow and Sanderson stage line started providing service; now the mail came in by stage on a regular basis.

Alonzo described his post office . . . *"it had a dirt roof, dirt floor, potbellied iron stove, and a box on the wall . . . men would gather around the hot little red stove and tell tales."* At this time, according to Hartman, there wasn't much mail . . . he claimed he could have carried it in his vest pocket. Alonzo would remain postmaster for the next nine years. In later years the crumbling old post office was restored and moved to its present location at Gunnison's Pioneer Museum.

In 1875, many miners and prospectors began to arrive in the Lake City and the San Juan areas. But another kind of settler was coming into the Gunnison Country at the same time as the miners – a significant number of "would be" ranchers. The vast reaches of grass (free grass) that grew in the valleys and hills were there for the taking, as were the homesteads that could be filed. The severe climate did not deter the hopefuls much, neither did the almost total lack of the existence of a town. Hartman, the first of this new breed of high altitude ranchers, welcomed the newcomers who, upon seeing his thriving operation, were heartened and readily took his advice on how to succeed. The following is an account of a few of the ranchers who came before the town was incorporated.

John B. Outcalt and his brother William had come to look over the Gunnison Country in 1874 with the Sylvester Richardson colony. They found the country a little cold for Richardson's proposed farming. And they found no other people except the crew at the cow camp on the Gunnison. They observed Hartman's operation and finding it successful, proceeded to secure property located four miles up the Gunnison River and soon were harvesting 500 tons of hay and had 1,100 acres of meadowland going. It was wild hay and they considered it as good as tame hay and stated that it only needed irrigation and then "the hay would grow itself." Then they turned their attention to raising cattle.

William Perry Sammons arrived in the Gunnison Country in 1876 riding a burro. He took a good look at quite a bit of the country, following Indian trails and fording streams to reach Taylor Park and then tracking into the Ohio Creek area. Here he describes in his memoirs river bottoms with rye grass as "high as a man's head." He had occasion to meet up with other of the earliest pioneers as he explored the country, among them John Outcalt, Professor Richardson, and of course, Alonzo Hartman. He reported seeing a very few sawed log houses, but few signs of civilization otherwise. He looked over the country to the south and was pleased with what he found there and put down stakes in the Powderhorn country and stayed for good.

Cyrus E. Crooks came into the country in May of 1877 – a failed gold miner from the eastern slope. He found the hay crop to his liking in the area where Needle Creek and the Tomichi River join about halfway between Doyleville and Sargents. He began to establish a ranch there – a ranch that, because of its location, quickly became a "road ranch" or stage stop. It would become a town of sorts in time, with a general store, a school, a section house for the railroad that was soon to come – even a saloon, maybe two.

In 1878 Rudolf Mergelman was born to August and Emma Mergelman a mile east of Iola on his parent's newly established ranch. His father had driven a mule team over the mountains into the Gunnison Country in 1875. Rudolf was one of the first white children born in the Gunnison Country. He would grow up and ranch on his birthplace for his entire life; his descendants thrive here today.

In 1879 A.K. and P.T. Stevens decided on Stueben Creek just west of Gunnison as a good location for a ranch and began encouraging a hay crop. This was observed by their only neighbors, Ute Indians, still summering in the valley. The Stevens' first job was to convince these Indian neighbors to not burn down their hay crop and convince them that it was being grown for horses to eat. It was surely the Ute's country first, but before long only arrowheads were left as evidence of this. It was the white man's ranching that would grow and thrive now on Stueben Creek.

In June of 1879, Mr. and Mrs. S.C. Fisher arrived in Gunnison driving a span of mules. They were accompanied by Mrs. Fisher's mother and eighty year-old grandmother who were driving a spring wagon. Mr. Fisher and a brother-in-law had preceded the women two weeks earlier – each driving freight wagons with ten-mule teams. When they arrived in Gunnison they found a town consisting of three log cabins and a frame house that served as a jail. They settled at the site of present day Almont, being the first to take up land at the confluence of the Taylor and East Rivers. Here they operated a toll bridge and engaged in the freighting business. Soon they turned to ranching with part of the family working at Jack's Cabin, a site near the East River and north of Almont, and part on Ohio Creek. Along with cattle, the Fisher family specialized in raising blooded horses.

While the Fisher family had arrived in the Gunnison country in style, most came with more modest means. Little Mamie McConnell Reppy walked into the country as her father had earlier done when he traveled the ninety some miles from Lake City to the Tomichi Valley on foot to take up a homestead. In 1879 his wife and children traveled to this new homestead from Missouri, traveling the latter half of the journey by covered wagon. Mamie recalled arriving in the valley on a very cold November night on foot – having been made to walk behind the wagon to keep warm. The dwelling that awaited the new arrivals was a rough cabin with a canvas serving the purpose of a door, a dirt floor, dirt roof, and the most essential item, the stove, missing. The McConnell family persevered – one of the first to settle at the foothills of Tomichi Dome, some 20 miles east of Gunnison, and begin the long tradition of ranching in the Tomichi Valley.

These were but a few of the pioneer ranchers who began to trickle into the Gunnison Country following the lead of Hartman and Richardson and with like intentions. Many of them had little or no experience in ranching, but some had at least a limited knowledge of farming. Elsewhere on the Western Slope, ranching was rapidly coming into existence, too. The mild winters of 1874 to 1878 made conditions for it optimal. Beef were now suddenly appearing where only deer and elk and buffalo had roamed before. The Western Slope was just beginning to be appreciated for its potential for the range cattle industry. The cowboy look had even arrived – a few were wearing buckskin with fringes, boots and spurs. Red bandannas and wide brimmed hats were now seen and often a ".32-20 special" holstered at the hip completed the "look."

Alonzo's wild empty country, only recently "Indian territory", was quickly turning into "cattle country." Alonzo Hartman, steadily working away to develop his own ranch, saw Gunnison slowly beginning to build up now and it wouldn't be too long before the creak of freight wagon wheels, the rumble of the stage coach, and the whistle of the train would drown out the wail of the lonesome coyote at the Dos Rios.

ABOUT ALFERD PACKER

At approximately the same time as the group of prospectors mentioned earlier arrived dog-tired at the cow camp in Gunnison, Alferd Packer led a group of five other prospectors out of Ouray's Delta winter camp. Instead of following the chief's instructions to track along the Gunnison River to the cow camp, they took a cut off which led them to the present-day Lake City area. Packer was not heard of again until early April when he walked into the Los Pinos Agency. He was exhausted but apparently in good health. Packer at first claimed to have no knowledge of the whereabouts of the five other men, having allegedly been separated from them at some point. Further questioning from a suspicious agent named Adams caused Packer to change his story. He next claimed that the five men, trapped near Lake City, had eaten one another to survive until only one man was left, a man Packer said he had to kill in self-defense. Shortly after his confrontation with Adams, Packer was imprisoned in the Saguache jail on suspicion of having been responsible for the murder and cannibalization of his companions. He escaped from jail but was later recaptured and returned to the Lake City and Gunnison areas. He was tried and convicted in 1886 in the Gunnison County Courthouse for the murder and cannibalism of his five companions. He was sentenced to forty years in prison and paroled in 1900, thenceforth always subject to much controversy and repulsion for his alleged acts – acts he steadfastly denied until his death in 1907.

Gunnison historian Duane Vandenbusche reports in his book "The Gunnison Country" that after Packer was sentenced a bartender ran to the nearest saloon and reported the following "erroneous" but popular version of the sentence:

"The judge says: Stand up, yah voracious man-eating son of a bitch, stand up. They was sivin Dimmicrats in Hinsdale County, and ye eat five of them,   God dam ye. I sintins ye t'be hanged by the neck until ye're dead, dead, dead, as a warnin' ag'in reducin' the Dimmicrat population of th' state."

Part IV

A Town Is Born

When the government cow camp closed down, Alonzo Hartman was twenty-five years old, hardened by the West, still a bachelor, and accustomed to the Gunnison Country's great isolation and sparse population. He undoubtedly watched with great interest and anticipation as the country slowly began to build up and new arrivals began to trickle in. Before much of a town was yet in existence, he was putting in endless hours of backbreaking work building up his homestead - converting it from its former wilderness state (that of wild grass and acres of sage brush and willows) into a productive working ranch. Alonzo always remained, at heart, a cattleman. But he would also, in time, take full advantage of any and all other opportunities he could find related to the development of the new town.

While Alonzo divided his time between carving a ranch out of the wilderness and acting as postmaster - between 1875 and 1879 - Gunnison began building up seriously. This was mainly due to a mining boom - to silver and gold discoveries in the surrounding country and the birth of several mining camps. Among them were White Pine, Pitkin, and Ohio City to the east and to the north, Gothic and Irwin and Crested Butte. In the Taylor Park area Tin Cup and Hillerton sprang up. These were but a few and the hub of activity for them all was the "just being born" town of Gunnison. Many toll roads had been built previously here and there and they provided routes into the new mining camps, crossing country that historically had been traversed only by Indian trails.

Agriculture, in the form of growing and selling hay (at the unheard of price of $35 to $40 a ton) was launched. Feed was desperately needed for the growing numbers of livestock and teams coming into the country, especially for the Barlow & Sanderson stage line's large numbers of horses. Beef was in great demand, needed to augment the monotonous fare of wild game that was often the only item on the menu of the early miners. The new mining camps supplied a lucrative market for the beef being raised by the country's brand new ranchers. Early on, Hartman supplied beef to Lake City's mining camps.

A half century later when writing his memoirs, Alonzo would recall – as if it were yesterday - the birth of the town of Gunnison. *"In 1879 the new town of Gunnison was formed by former Governor John Evans, Henry C. Olney, editor of Lake City Silver World, Louden Mullin, Sylvester Richardson, and me. 160 acres were set aside for the town. . . By 1880 there was a tent city with 500 men. The town was incorporated March 1, 1880. By May people were pouring into the country – by August two hundred buildings were constructed – but many tents still existed."*

Another early Gunnison resident, George Root, was quoted in the July 20, 1939 – *Gunnison News Champion*. He recalled that in 1880 the "Gunnison boom" occurred. By very early spring, there were 500 people camping west of town. On the town site were forty-five buildings and thirty-eight tents. By May there were even more tents put up and more new buildings underway. One visitor to the town counted 1500 wagons between Pueblo and Gunnison – most headed for Gunnison. A town jail – one story - was hastily constructed to house the lawless that could always be counted on to arrive at every frontier boom town. Alonzo's post office, by then moved to town, often had a line that extended far into the street. Hundreds of burros brayed all night long attended by the yelping of scores of "worthless dogs." A heavy growth of sagebrush covered the town site. Root mentioned, as did many others who wrote of this time, the great numbers of sage chickens running about the tents and buildings and into the streets and through the sagebrush. Others referred to Gunnison at this time as a "prairie dog town."

Many of the arrivals to the new town of Gunnison in 1880-81 came by covered wagon by way of Saguache to the southeast or Salida across the Divide. Some of the new arrivals traveled alone on horseback; a few on foot, and many by freight wagon. They found Gunnison like most other frontier towns – rough and primitive, but beginning to show the promise of civilization. There was a newspaper and a crude water supply coursing in ditches down either side of the wide main street. A courthouse was about to be constructed and there were numerous boarding houses, restaurants and log buildings amid the many residential tents. A bank had opened in May, a killing or two had taken place, and more than one sermon had been preached. A few Ute Indians could be found on the streets wandering among the townspeople. Saloons, gambling houses, and red light districts were numerous, but there were also plans underway for schools and churches, promoted by the more civilly inclined. By 1881 the population had reached approximately 3,000 with many still camping alongside the Gunnison River upon arrival. About this time the city, with its eye on even further development, financed the

An early 1880s photo of Gunnison's Main Street looking north. The Hartman Building is second from left.

WSCU Archives

Gunnison Main Street in 2012 looking north from Tomichi Ave. Hartman Building is second from left.

Walt Barron Photo

extension of Alonzo's '75 ditch. The ditch would cut across some eight miles of ranch land to the new town and irrigate several hay meadows along the way. With the arrival of Hartman's water, many trees were planted along the streets.

The Barlow and Sanderson stage arrived in the summer of 1880, a double line of four-horse stage coaches ran from Salida to Gunnison. These legendary stage coaches of the Old West rumbled through the Gunnison Country on a regular basis until August 1882, and then passed into history when the trains arrived. But in its prime the overland stage was bringing in passengers – four at a time – over Marshall Pass and then networking into all the major mining camps in the area, with up to twenty stages arriving daily. A great many horses were needed for the 10 to 25-mile run and changes of four and six horse teams.

An early-day Gunnison train.
Western State Colorado University Archives –
Savage Library

The demise of the stage was brought about by William Jackson Palmer who brought his Denver and Rio Grande narrow gauge to the town, crossing Marshall Pass from Salida and reaching Gunnison in August of 1881. Local pioneers celebrated for days and surely Alonzo and his recent cow camp partner Jim Kelly were foremost among them, amazed at how their former country was changing. Soon to follow the heralded D&RG was the Denver, South Park and Pacific, coming from Denver and climbing to the crest of the Continental Divide where it tunneled through at the famed Alpine Tunnel and on to Gunnison, soon branching north to the coal mines at Baldwin up Ohio Creek. The Alpine Tunnel was a 1,700-foot narrow gauge tunnel from which a precarious descent was constructed into the Quartz Creek Valley.

After the coming of the two railroads and the increase in population, Alonzo, still postmaster, had a salary increase to $3,000 a year. He began building up wealth in other ways, too. He sold easements to the new railroads and used the profits to buy more land to increase the size of the Dos Rios. He took full advantage of Gunnison's new mode of transportation, stating, "*Of course, the coming of the two railroads in 1881 and 1882 made life much easier. The Alpine Tunnel let me get my cattle to Denver in one day, saving on feed and lost weight. Ranching became a great deal more profitable then.*" He was right, of course, the coming of the railroad cinched it for the local cattlemen. Ranching would now become a much more viable operation. The early markets had been mainly mining camps, but with the coming of the railroad other markets opened up and when Denver buyers offered prices for beef that weren't good enough there were markets east, such as- Omaha and Kansas City.

Alonzo and the other ranchers increased their herds now and began shipping cattle out in great numbers. In the late fall Alonzo's cattle were sent to Denver. He would usually order some twenty cars, each car holding twenty head of cattle. More than this would call for an extra engine. He would go as far as Salida with his cattle and oversee the transfer of them from the narrow gauge to the broad gauge train. He was always on hand for the transfer, claiming that the rail hands were too rough on his livestock. He stayed in Salida overnight, sometimes sleeping in the lobby of the Palace hotel, and continue on to Denver the next day on a passenger train. At Denver, commission buyers would be on hand to wine and dine Alonzo and the other Gunnison stockmen. It was customary for them to wile away the time waiting for the cattle to arrive by drinking -- "feeling no pain," as they put it – it was tradition. It is unknown whether Alonzo participated in the "tradition" but after his cattle arrived and the sale was completed he would be paid with a check on the spot. Then, after having had a brief taste of a more cosmopolitan life, he would board the train and head back to the isolated Gunnison Country and the Dos Rios Ranch.

While increasingly busy with the enlargement of the Dos Rios and the sale of many cattle, Alonzo also continued with his job as postmaster. By now he had a new location on Main Street, although it was still a log cabin. This was soon replaced by a more substantial brick building, the opening of which is described by Alonzo: "*On*

December 1, 1881, we christened my brick post office building on Main Street by a dance given by the young people. It was called by the newspaper the finest building in the city, it was two stories high, and cost $4,500. Many invitations were issued for the dance, and a large crowd, composed of Gunnison's best society was present. There was excellent music, and the dancing was kept up till a later hour." Alonzo goes on to describe other new developments in the town: *"Now there was a new brick bank on Main Street, and I became first vice-president in 1881."* The Board of Directors of this new bank consisted of the famed H.A.W. Tabor of First National Bank of Denver, other Colorado bankers, and locals S.G. Gill and Hartman.

The courthouse was also built at this time and among the new employees was one who would change the course of Alonzo's bachelor life. He remembers, *"In it, as assistant in the office of the county clerk, worked a young woman – an almost unheard of thing in those times. Her name was Annie Leah Haigler . . . we soon became good friends and then engaged to be married. As an old bachelor of 32, I came in for a lot of joking from my friends. Annie and I lived in the cabin at Dos Rios for a while, but driving back and forth to the post office in all kinds of weather was hard. And ranch life was lonely for Annie. I had 1,080 acres then and could find plenty of intelligent men to work for me . . . so I bought some lots on Wisconsin Street and built a house of white building stone."* The new house was built in 1883 -84 on the southwest corner of Denver and Wisconsin Streets. Earlier, In1879, several other lots on Wisconsin Street had been platted and sold by a company owned by Alonzo and Sylvester Richardson. An almost identical sandstone house was built near Alonzo and Annie's new house by master stone mason, Fred Zugelder in 1880, and it is very likely that Zugelder built Alonzo's

71

also. (At the writing of this book, both houses survive.) Alonzo owned several other lots around Gunnison including, he claimed, the land that the Courthouse was built on. The "Hartman Building," on Main Street, an Italian style edifice with arched windows, which still exists today, was built in 1881.

Alonzo and Annie were married in 1882 and from that time on for the next several years, the town continued to grow and Alonzo, whose main occupation was still ranching, became one of its most prominent citizens and continued to be involved with the advancements of the town. The *News Champion* on March 20, 1882, according to Alonzo, boasted: *"From a town inhabited only by prairie dogs Gunnison is now a metropolis of 4,000 busy people, 5 churches, 2 schoolhouses, 4 hotels, and stores and business houses filled with goods that would be a credit to a city of 25,000."* Other new developments in the town included a "Poor House" in 1881 and a telephone system that was established by 1882. The town could now even boast of having as residents a couple of famous gunfighters.

Wyatt Earp and Doc Holliday arrived in the fledgling town of Gunnison in 1882, not long after the famed "gunfight at the O.K. Corral." They first camped on the outskirts of town, west along the Gunnison River. Their arrival to the town was duly noted by the press. Local citizens were well aware of their reputations. Both had earned their membership in a very select group – they were among the top ten gunfighters in the West. Although he does not mention it in his memoirs, Alonzo very likely knew them. Wyatt stayed in Gunnison for a year or so, running a faro game in a ramshackle two-story building on the second block of Main Street–probably getting his mail from Alonzo's nearby post office. Earp and Holliday caused no trouble during their stay and soon moved on continuing their habit of wandering through the West's many boomtowns, investing in mines and running gambling establishments.

Alonzo had been in the country for little more than a decade when he witnessed the construction of the La Veta Hotel – a structure that must have seemed truly magnificent when compared to his abode of only a short few years before – the primitive log cabin at the cow camp, Construction was started in 1881, and completed in 1884 at a cost of $200,000. The La Veta was located on the then fashionable South Boulevard Street. When completed it was the epitome of a fine hotel with a large staff and elaborate furnishings. The local newspaper described a building of Queen Anne architecture four stories high with elegant black walnut furniture everywhere throughout, a bar backed by the largest plate glass mirror in Colorado, and a total of one hundred exquisite sleeping rooms. The La Veta was formally opened on May 22, 1884. Four hundred guests, attired in their best, attended in "fancy gowns for the ladies" and "many brought out wedding coats for the men." Annie's gown was described in the local newspaper as "a foulard with a taupe background figured in rose." (This gown and Alonzo's wedding coat are now on display at Gunnison's Pioneer Museum.) Dinner - a far cry from Alonzo's former cow camp fare – was served on tables with white table cloths and fine silver and china. The dinner was followed by a dance and the first dance, the Grand March, was led by two of Gunnison's foremost citizens of the day, Alonzo and Annie Hartman. It was all pretty fancy for a place still only a step removed from Indian Territory, Alonzo may have thought, and the grizzly bear and mountain lion still roamed nearby.

Annie Hartman's dress, worn at the grand opening of the La Veta Hotel in May of 1884. Now on display at the Gunnison Pioneer Museum.

Walt Barron Photo

Alonzo's wedding suit, left, and his smoking jacket with an early photo of Hartman at approximately age 30. On display at the Gunnison Pioneer Museum.

Walt Barron Photo   75

The La Veta Hotel, circa 1884.

WSCU Archives – Savage Library

The hotel's sitting room, circa 1884.

WSCU Archives – Savage Library

Part V

Cattle
Country

Hartman, new to such positions as vice president of the bank or leader of the Grand March at the La Veta, performed these functions not only well but with a new gentlemanly sophistication. He was, however, still most at home in the saddle and on the range. He watched as the new decade of the 1880s brought in more and more ranchers to the valley, watched as much of the valley bottom land was taken up by homesteads and saw the summer ranges populated by ever-growing numbers of cattle.

Alonzo observed his neighbor ranchers' efforts and saw their early hard work show steady promise. Ranches grew and began to prosper. The dishonest, the impatient, the inept, and the unlucky of the pioneer ranchers did not make it in the business for long, however, nor did the faint of heart. Alonzo and the others who made it, had be tough and persistent. But toughness alone wasn't enough. Know-how about high altitude ranching was yet to be developed and knowledge of the climate and soil was new and sketchy. Many looked to Alonzo for advice as he seemed to have figured out how to make his operation succeed in this, the severest of climates. Even so, as Alonzo would undoubtedly have acknowledged, a gambler's courage was needed to start in the first place.

Fortunately for them all, the pioneer rancher's gamble was staked by the government through the various homestead acts, the ones Alonzo had already taken advantage of. Having staked out his first 160-acre claim he had, in fact, also established grazing rights – unwritten rights on unfenced range – understood by his neighbors who were surviving by the same methods, their cattle and horses intermingled on the free range as their numbers grew. At the home ranches meadows were now producing as much as three tons of hay per acre and by 1885 huge numbers of cattle, wintered on the excess hay and summered on the superb high altitude range grass, were being shipped out of Gunnison by the hundreds – by the thousands.

And while all this sounds good, it was never going to be easy. Newly claimed land was usually blanketed with sagebrush and willows. The work put in to clear this land was staggering, done by men, women, and children and often done by hand. Sometimes an easier method used to clear sagebrush was the pulling of several yards of huge chain links (ships anchor) between four teams of horses. Ditches had to be dug to bring water where water had not been before. The main ones were wide and deep - the many, many smaller ones networked out like arteries and veins. Overwhelming amounts of work went into constructing these ditches, testing the endurance of both man and beast. Smaller ones were dug by hand – no small feat on a large acreage. Bigger ditches could be dug with the help of horse power and the use of a "slip" or a "fresno."

In the earliest days, as Gunnison ranching became more and more successful and before the establishment of the Forest Reserves, there was enormous competition for open range and blatant overuse resulted. Much overgrazing occurred locally in the late 1800s and the early 1900s as cattlemen overstocked the range not only with cattle but with horses as well. (Early ranchers owned great numbers of horses, some having as many as fifty to seventy-five head.) According to old timers, in the early days, as many as 10,000 cattle summered in Taylor Park and as many as 5,000 in the upper Ohio Creek area. In 1891, in response to excessive forest cutting and grazing across the West, forest lands were withdrawn from the public domain and grazing, mining, and timber cutting were prohibited, at least temporarily. Initially these new restrictions, now placed on Gunnison's ranchers, were bearable. There was still much public domain that was administered by the General Land Office (later the Bureau of Land Management). It was unregulated and available for free grazing until 1934 when the Taylor Grazing Act passed. Moreover, in the beginning there was little enforcement of the new regulations. The "law of the west" still pretty much prevailed. As one former Gunnison Forest Ranger put it, "the firstest got the mostest."

On May 12, 1905 the reserves became national forests under Theodore Roosevelt's presidency. Twenty-one new forests with an estimated forty million acres were established including the Gunnison National Forest. Alonzo and other local ranchers saw the government's assertion of authority over public lands as a threat to their traditional claims to the use of the range as well as an encouragement to sheep men to move into established cattle ranges. The free range days were over for Gunnison's cattlemen as eighty percent of Gunnison County's land came under federal control and regulation. Cattlemen were enraged by the new grazing fees – the concept of charging fees for grazing prevailed, however, and was eventually accepted. There were those among the local cattlemen's association members who actually supported the concept, provided it had a definite maximum, and they openly accused some of their contemporaries of being "hostile." It is not known were Hartman stood in this matter, although it *is* known that his designated grazing area was to remain Taylor Park.

A major part of Alonzo's ranching operation was in connection with Taylor Park. Since 1860 placer mining had been going on here and there in the park and also in nearby Union Park. By 1879 towns like Tin Cup and Hillerton were established. Primitive roads had been built early-on over Cottonwood Pass (from Buena Vista and Leadville) and other passes, into the Taylor Park area and a freight and stage service established, along with the first newspaper, the *Hillerton Occident.* Most of the newcomers flocking in had "gold fever" and looked at the park as a place that provided tremendous promise for mining, but in Alonzo's and the other rancher's eyes, what Taylor Park and Union Park provided was one of the finest cattle ranges in all of Colorado.

Taylor Park lies to the east of the East River Valley on County Road 742. It was once, before the building of the reservoir, a high grassy basin some 30 miles long by 8 miles wide. Early-on herds of buffalo had grazed in this remote park in grass up to their bellies. Taylor Park is mountain locked; peaks on the east form the Continental Divide and the spectacular Collegiate Peaks rise to the northeast. Mountains ranging up to 13,000 feet loom in nearly every direction. A beautiful, smaller open park - Union Park lies a few miles to the south of Taylor Park.

The Union Park cow camp as it appeared in 1994.

Walt Barron Photo

Remains of the camp in Hartman's Gulch, midway between Gunnison and Taylor Park.

Gib Kysar Photo (2012)

Alonzo's ever growing cattle herd, as well as those of his neighbors further up Tomichi and Quartz Creek summered here in the park, miles away from their home ranches. In about 1900 a "pool" of ranchers was organized to oversee the grazing of these intermingled cattle herds in the park. The new "Taylor Park Cattle Pool" hired riders to watch over the cattle in the summer and all participating ranchers did duty in the fall round-up.

The late Paul Vader, Gunnison rancher and grandson of pioneer Palmer Vader, who had early-on teamed up with Hartman to graze cattle in the park, described the fall roundup: *"In the early days . . . camp supplies, grub, stock salt, etc., were hauled to the Taylor Park cow camps by chuck wagons usually drawn by four horses. The water supply was taken by bucket from a nearby spring or stream. The Majestic, Home Comfort, or other wood cook stove had a handy reservoir attached for heating water . . . if a bath was needed, one merely dipped water out of the reservoir and put it in a galvanized, cylindrical vessel called a number three wash tub . . . On the first day of the fall roundup we butchered a beef to eat. We quartered it and kept it in a large, screened cooler on the side of the cabin. When the roundup ended ten days later it was virtually all eaten."*

Pool riders and round-up participants stayed at a camp called Pie Plant in Taylor Park, which was located north of the present-day reservoir. Another camp existed in Union Park and was somewhat isolated from the public, tucked away in an area where there not much traffic. It was originally a dwelling used by placer miners, searching for ore on Lottis Creek and other nearby streams. This cabin remains and has been used by the Taylor Park Pool since the early 1900s. The original character of the building – a long succession of rooms – has been preserved by a recent repair job. Visiting there now, one finds a scene not far removed from what Alonzo knew a hundred years ago.

Former Gunnison rancher, Gib Kysar, who had a grazing permit in Taylor Park for many years and was, as well, the Taylor Park Cattle Pool's "range boss" for a number of years was an attentive listener as the "old timers" told tales at the fall roundups. He provided much interesting information on the camp's history. According to several of these "old timers," Alonzo was in the park well before the Forest Reserves were established and had, in fact, broken the trail into Taylor Canyon. The route into Union Park used by Hartman began at his Dos Rios Ranch which lay west of the present Gold Basin Road. Enroute to Taylor Park Alonzo drove his cattle north through the town of Gunnison to Sleepy Hollow (now Cranor Hill Road) and then on up Lost Canyon, following an Indian trail. Later on, various other routes into Taylor Park were used by the ranchers located further east on Tomichi and Quartz creeks, but all trails eventually converged in the upper end of Beaver Creek (where Hartman's mid-trip overnight cabin was located and which remains to this day). From here cattle were pushed straight forward northerly along the sides of Beaver Creek (a tributary of the Taylor River), to the confluence of the two rivers (at present day Harmel's Resort) and on to a point in Taylor River Canyon named "One Mile Draw," then to the Taylor River, traversing on to the junction of Taylor River and Lottis Creek, and from there going through Lottis Creek Canyon into Union Park.

The breed of government cattle that Alonzo first trailed into the parks in the early 1870s were probably a mix and match of Longhorn, Shorthorn and Durham – as were the cattle of most other early-day ranchers in the area and the state. These early cattle looked much different than cattle today. They were longer of leg, narrower of back and smaller in the hindquarters. This conformation enabled them to travel well for long distances – a requirement of the pioneer era cattle. Often, after ranching started to flourish in the Gunnison Country, these early cattle were trailed in from as far away as Utah or over Marshall Pass or Cochetopa Pass from the San Luis Valley. With enough bad luck, one of these early trail drives to Gunnison could take a month and required a cow that was up to the rigors of the trip. A change took place by the turn of the century or shortly thereafter, with the gradual replacement of the old time cattle breeds with the "white faces" – the Herefords. These beautiful English cattle made their mark in the Gunnison Country and in much of the rest of the West as well. For many years most local herds were predominately Hereford. They were a hardy breed which could meet the demands of survival in a savagely cold climate and exist on huge shared rangelands without close attention which was common practice in the Gunnison Country.

Alonzo branding at the Dos Rios Ranch in 1900.

Bruce Hartman Photo

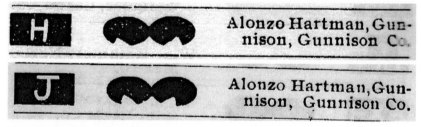

Two brands and earmarks registered by Alonzo and reproduced in "The Colorado Brand Book" of 1900 "Containing all stock brands on file in the Office of Secretary of State up to and including August 31, 1900."

Courtesy of the Publisher

Alonzo along with other local ranchers soon saw the need to organize. The local cattlemen's association, patterned after the Colorado Cattleman's Association, was established in June of 1894. Faded ink on century-old ledgers record the cattlemen's first items of business. Various battles and resolutions, sometimes deliberately understated, are the subject matter of the early records.

Their purpose was: influencing the territorial and state legislatures to pass laws that were in the cattlemen's interest, dealing with the growing issues of the control of grass and water rights, organizing roundups, overseeing branding and assisting with the critical issues of the control of cattle disease and cattle rustling. By now, an old hand at the ranching business and highly successful, forty-four year-old Hartman was elected first president of the group.

"The ranchers organized in 1894." Alonzo recalls in his memoirs, *"They called it the Gunnison Cattlemen's Association, and elected me their first president. We decided to have a Cattlemen's Celebration every year, with racing, wild horse breaking, roping, horse quadrilles, bulldogging and granite drilling by men from the Aberdeen quarry . . . At first we had the events up and down Main Street, but later we made a race course and grandstand so we could charge admission and have money for prizes."*

An early Cattleman's Day parade (probably around 1900).
Bruce Hartman photo

Other typical cattlemen's concerns across the west around the turn of the century, besides such things as summer rodeos, were the increasing "invasion" of sheep into what the cattlemen deemed "their" claim on the range. This issue deeply concerned Alonzo too, and he explained the situation: "*A feud as deadly as that between the Montagues and Capulets existed for years between the cattlemen and sheepmen. Both depended upon the public domain for pasture, and the cattlemen insisted that cows would not eat where 'them stinking sheep had been or drink where they had dirtied the water.' Such a situation led to mob law, and many gruesome tales were told. So hot did the fight become that Uncle Sam sent to all the Western States for delegates to talk things over. I was one of the delegates, and a very warm discussion we had. Finally the sheepmen in Gunnison were allotted the high range where the brush they liked was plentiful, and the cattlemen were allowed the foothills, in early spring, the grassy mountain slopes after June 15. Each rancher was assigned a certain range and required to keep a herder with the cattle constantly. I was given a section on Taylor River.*"

Long before the agreement that Alonzo describes above took place, the West's infamous sheep and cattle wars were to visit the Gunnison area in a major way. Local cattlemen were convinced that the "trespassing" sheep would overgraze and destroy the range and, as a result, three major sheep killings occurred in the area. Alonzo either witnessed one of these or more likely was a participant in one. (The "code of silence" on this matter has kept the names of the participants more or less secret for decades.) But according to the recollections of one of Alonzo's hired cowboys of that time, Tom Crews, Alonzo Hartman, a known sheep hater, called for the young cowboys in his hire to gather horses at midnight one night at the Dos Rios. He then took all of the men and horses up Lost Canyon Road for a rendezvous with Tomichi Creek ranchers and the bunch then rode over to the Taylor River into Taylor Park assumedly to teach an invading sheep herder a lesson.

It was the summer of 1904 and one of the hated migratory sheep men, even knowing he was courting trouble, could not resist the vast reaches of grass growing in the park. Surely there was enough to go around. B.F. Saunders, a Utah sheep baron moved into Taylor Park in late June, just as it was greening up into prime condition. He entered the park from the north coming across Taylor Pass from near Aspen with a huge flock of some 5,000 sheep. He was not welcomed warmly, especially after indicating that he was prepared to bring in thousands more sheep if he found no trouble with the cattlemen that summer. But trouble found him instead, and very shortly, in the form of 100 masked men armed with green aspen clubs, and rifles. They found the invader near Dorchester, at the north end of the park and ran about 1,500 of his sheep into a corral where they were clubbed and shot to death. No stockman was ever found out. To this day it is unknown with any certainty if Hartman was involved.

In later years sheep were grazed again in the higher elevations of Taylor Park while the cattle were grazed at lower elevations.

Although preoccupied from time to time by sheep wars, civic duties, and of course, his growing family, Alonzo faithfully kept on with his ranching venture into his 60's. He increased his original 160 acres to 2,000 acres, eventually owning one of the most prominent ranches in Colorado. The Dos Rios included miles of streams that offered some of the finest fishing anywhere. He branched out, buying and selling large numbers of cattle, some selling as far away as South Africa. Eventually he built a fish hatchery which he operated for a few years, believing he should supplement what had been the bountiful supply of trout he had first found in the Gunnison and Tomichi Rivers. For a time he and his son operated a dairy and sold dairy products. He kept up with his town activities and obligations, too, even serving a term as county commissioner.

By 1910, for almost forty years Alonzo had watched a desolate, isolated, and unpopulated, though beautiful valley slowly blossom and grow. He had bid his friends the Utes goodbye and had seen newcomers take their place. He had started with a little 160-acre homestead and built it into an empire of land and cattle, all the while helping in a major way to build up a new frontier town. He had built a mansion and raised a family. He had evolved from a rough cowboy into a distinguished gentleman rancher and he had watched as the countryside evolved too, from the former acres of willow and sage into lush hay meadows - into beautiful, bountiful country - splendid cattle country in its prime.

* * *

Alonzo Hartman was involved in a court case in the early 1900s that eventually went to the Supreme Court of Colorado in 1905. This case has since had a significant bearing on the law concerning the right to float down a stream that traverses the property of another. This issue, which so infuriated Hartman, is still inflammatory with private landowners today and there is still a considerable amount of dissention over the subject. Hartman's case has been cited many times since in support of land owners' rights related to floaters' rights and is still the law in Colorado.

The District Court of Gunnison County, first heard this case brought by Hartman. The judgment was for the defendant, a man named Tresise. The case concerned a claim by Hartman, who stated that his property was enclosed by a fence and posted and that the defendant forcibly broke and entered, knowing of the posting and having been personally notified by Hartman not to enter and fish in the natural stream. The court dismissed the action on the grounds that the citizens of the state have the constitutional and statutory right to fish in natural streams against the wish and protest of the owner of the land through which the streams flow when the waters thereof have been stocked with fish at public expense. In 1905 the Supreme Court reversed this decision stating that ownership of the stream bed was held to include the exclusive right of fishery in waters flowing over it . . . whoever "breaks the close" intrudes upon the space above the surface of the land without permission from the owner, whether it be for fishing or other recreational purposes, and commits a trespass.

Dos Rios Memories

Part VI

A Man's Home Is His Castle

Gunnison never did become the metropolis that many had expected it to be during the mining boom. The higher grade ore had been taken early and eventually many mines closed down and Gunnison's growth slowed to a halt. By the mid-1880s many buildings in town stood empty and people were leaving. Daily newspapers became weekly and in time the La Veta Hotel, built in anticipation of great things to come, closed its doors in the winter months. Things revived again around 1895 as coal mines became big producers, able to prosper by being able to ship coal out by train. There were several gold strikes made south of town to add somewhat to the area's prosperity. But while the growth of the town may have slowed down, things never did slow down for Alonzo Hartman and the others in the cattle business. They had discovered where the real gold turned out to be – the free grass in the nearby hills - and Hartman, willing to put in the colossal amount of work required, would lead the rest in taking advantage of it. The late 1800s and early 1900s were bonanza years for the local cattlemen and Alonzo became wealthy.

With his original 160 acre tract of land still part of the ranch, he had, by 1905, increased his holdings to two thousand acres. The ranch yielded some fifteen hundred tons of hay a year, had extensive pasture lands, fine modern barns, sheds, and other structures. Always a "horse man" Alonzo took to raising blooded horses at this time. Among them was a stallion, a race horse that won scores of races and when retired was bred to Morgan mares, producing a cross that resulted in beautiful driving teams that Alonzo sold to the town folks. By the turn of the century he was considered one of the most prominent cattlemen on the Western Slope of Colorado, raising, buying, and selling very large numbers of cattle.

Throughout most of his 35-year thriving career in the cattle business, Alonzo had the advantage of having what he considered "*a first-rate partner*" – his wife, Annie. An "*old bachelor of thirty-two*" at the time of his marriage, Alonzo seemed to easily shift from his accustomed bachelor status to that of devoted husband and family man. It cannot be said that he chose a young, blushing bride for a mate. Annie Haigler was twenty-nine years old when she married Alonzo, at a time when unmarried women of that age were generally considered to be in the spinster category. Diminutive, small boned Annie was never a beauty, but although somewhat plain, she was still attractive. Alonzo claimed that he and Annie took time to become good friends, then liking what he saw, he soon married her. He claimed that she, like himself, was "always working" and this seemed to please him. Other accounts of Annie say that she was "blessed with a sunny disposition and a never-failing smile and radiated cheer to all her associates." Alonzo and Annie's marriage lasted nearly sixty years and the always fragile looking Annie lived well into her nineties.

Annie Haigler, born in 1853, was a native of West Virginia and the daughter of William P. and Mary (Hinkle) Haigler. The family members were westward-moving pioneers, as the Hartman family had been. They had moved by covered wagon from West Virginia to Kansas in 1860 when Annie was a child. Later on Annie became a graduate of a small college in Kansas, and was certified to become a teacher. Annie then taught pioneer children in the one-room schools of the day in rural Kansas. Annie's real love, however, was painting and by any standards she was a talented artist. After marriage (which ended her teaching career) she often escaped from family duties to pursue this passion. At some point in her teaching career in Kansas she suffered from health problems (the cause of which is now unknown) and her doctor advised to go to Colorado for her health. Annie must not have been seriously ill, however, for after her arrival in Gunnison she began working at the newly built Courthouse where she had a job as assistant to the county clerk. It was here that she caught the eye of the town's most eligible bachelor.

The wedding took place on January 29, 1882 at the home of Annie's parents in Monticello, Kansas. The couple returned to Gunnison, not taking time for a honeymoon. Alonzo brought his bride back to his homestead and a cabin at Dos Rios. Shortly after their return they were feted at a reception at the Mullin House which, according to Alonzo's memoirs, *"lasted till about midnight and was followed by supper, then dancing - a banquet was served, and many gifts received – it was as large a gathering as ever was assembled in Gunnison."*

If there was a picture taken at Annie and Alonzo's wedding, it does not now exist. They did, however, have a formal photograph taken the day before the wedding. Alonzo, looking handsome in his wedding suit, appears to tower over Annie. She is dressed in the fashion of the day when women wore dresses with bustles, cinched in their waists to tiny sizes with corsets, wore many petticoats, and finished up the look with high-buttoned shoes. Annie is dressed in a fur trimmed coat for this pre-wedding occasion and leans toward Alonzo as she did ever after in most of the pictures taken of them. Even in later years when they were elderly, tiny, frail Annie, coming up only to Alonzo's shoulder, would appear to lean against her husband, he always appearing straight, lean, and strong, handsome as ever in his later years.

Nothing is said in Hartman's memoirs of the year or so spent at the rustic cabin at the Dos Rios. The cabin, like most others at this time, was undoubtedly drafty and poorly heated. Plumbing in such early dwellings was nonexistent and outhouses served the purpose of bathrooms. A washtub in the kitchen sufficed for weekly baths. Annie, due to her own pioneer upbringing, was probably used to such accommodations, as was Alonzo. The problem, Alonzo claimed, was that Annie was lonely at the ranch, so he began drawing up plans for a new stone house to be built on a lot he owned on Wisconsin Street in Gunnison. Until it was built, Annie could be seen driving her horse-drawn buggy to town to find some friendly society and perhaps visit Alonzo at the post office.

The small, two story sandstone Wisconsin Street house where Annie and Alonzo lived from approximately

1883/84 until 1886 was a substantial home for the time in Gunnison, but the town itself was still pretty primitive. Boardwalk sidewalks and dirt streets were the norm and mud was terrible in the spring. Transportation was strictly by horse drawn buggies and wagons. The horses required to pull the vehicles of the day made a huge mess of the streets, adding to the mud. Popular songs of the day such as "In the Good Old Summertime" had to apply to Gunnison's short summer and "In the Shade of the Old Apple Tree" didn't apply at all.

While their new home in town was under construction, Annie and Alonzo took a delayed honeymoon and attended The World's Fair in Chicago. Alonzo had shipped five carloads of beef cattle to sell in Omaha and then he and Annie attended the fair and saw, as Alonzo remembered, *"all the sights – there were so many things to see that I forgot half of them."* Among the other wonders of that time, they witnessed the gigantic Ferris wheel that rose to fantastic heights and observed the miracle of the new invention of electrical lights. One can almost picture the honeymooning couple strolling through the Fair in their Victorian clothes – flush with money from Alonzo's sale of cattle in Omaha, taking in the sights. Here in Chicago, they bought a houseful of furniture and shipped it to Colorado for the new stone house under construction in Gunnison.

The Hartman's first child, Hazel Helen was born in 1884 shortly before the completion of the new house. Annie, now thirty years old, may have given birth to this first child at the cabin at Dos Rios, although that is now unknown – the birth may also have taken place at some location in town. Childbirth was a sometimes precarious proposition at this time and quite a few mothers did not survive the experience. Annie apparently fared well, though, and may have even been attended by a physician as was the custom for more well-to-do patients of this era. If so, chloroform was likely administered to ease the process. In 1886 the Hartman family, now living in the new stone house, welcomed their second child into the world - Bruce Alonzo Hartman.

Shortly after the birth of his son, Alonzo, possibly thinking that he needed to return to affairs at the ranch, built a second home. This new frame house was built at Dos Rios in 1886, and by some accounts was the first frame house in Gunnison. It was situated just behind the location of the famed "Hartman Castle" which was to be built in the future. It was painted a bright yellow and had brown trim and a shingle roof. Here and there and on the gables was a fashionable bit of gingerbread trim. By 1889 a huge and substantial brick barn was added to the collection of ranch structures, its date of inception on the keystone at the top of the barn. This structure was unfortunately gutted by fire a few years later. After living in the frame house for several years, their wealth increasing, Alonzo and Annie came up with the idea of building a more substantial home - one that henceforth would be generally referred to as "the Hartman Castle." It far outshone any other home in the community at this time and spoke as a symbol of the stature that Alonzo had achieved in the cattle business.

Most of the work involved in building the "castle" was done by local talent. A Gunnison minister – possibly Alonzo's and Annie's pastor - designed the house which was patterned after the Victorian style of the day and when completed, it was an elegant structure indeed. Locals were hired to add the many special touches to the house, including intricate brick work, a three story winding staircase, and fireplaces in several rooms, An unusual feature of the house was that the kitchen was in the basement - food was prepared there and then brought up on a dumbwaiter. This kitchen in the basement had low ceilings; it was (and is) rather dark and gloomy, but at the time it was cheered with a fireplace. The beautiful white oak curved staircase descended to this basement kitchen, connecting it with the first floor entrance hall and then wound on up to the second floor. The second floor had three bedrooms and a bathroom – a rarity at the time. On the landing or hall at the top of the stairs was a door that opened out onto a second story balcony. Also in this hall was a pull down staircase that led to the belvedere or turret and Annie's studio. Here, after pulling up the stairs, she would paint undisturbed for hours. On the west wall of this turret, for many years was a waterfall scene painted by her, showing her skills as a landscape artist.

Upon entering the "castle" (then and now) one first sees the magnificent oak staircase - the balustrades forming an S-shaped design. Climbing the staircase, stained glass windows ascend the wall, decreasing in size as one goes up the stairs. At the top of the stairs the colored glass windows feature flowers and owls. There are arches over several downstairs doors - made of wood filigree and scrollwork. In addition to the fancy filigree and parquet floors, and other embellishments, the house had several very new and modern conveniences for the time: hot running water, an elevator installed for use by the elder relatives who would henceforth always live with the Hartmans, water pumped into the house by use of a windmill, and a huge new cooking range with a hot water jacket on the side of the stove.

The Hartmans furnished their new home with walnut pieces and Annie painted murals in the upstairs hallway. The Italian marble statues which were part of the fireplace art work they had purchased at the World's Fair peeked out from a downstairs fireplace. When finished, this elegant house hardly had the look of the typical western "ranch house," like those built by other wealthy cattlemen of the era, but it certainly had "western touches." The Italian pieces and Annie's murals were joined by a collection of Ute Indian artifacts. This included gifts from Alonzo's earlier days at Los Pinos and gifts from Chief Ouray and Chipeta. The stately house was soon encircled with a fence, not the popular fancy iron fence of the day that one would have expected, but a fence made of elk and deer antlers – piles of them – arches of them. And of course the "castle" was closely neighbored by the barns, corrals, and bunkhouses of the Dos Rios, hitching posts placed strategically among them.

The house, built in 1891, reportedly cost $45,000, an unheard of amount at the time. Alonzo, Annie, their two children, and Annie's mother, Mary Haigler and possibly some servants moved in on Christmas Day.

The castle was a busy happy family home for the Hartman's for twenty or more years. The Hartman children grew up here. Alonzo was a generous man and during these two decades the household almost always included several other people, including for this entire time, Annie's mother and eventually Alonzo's mother too - Mary Boone Hartman. Both of these women had known many pioneering hardships and the castle must have seemed like a dream to them. Others, perhaps friends or relatives, lived in the castle from time to time as is evidenced by census reports. Servants generally lived in the original frame house behind the castle, now known as the "carriage house."

Bruce and Hazel were in their early teens when a baby sister, Leah Louise, arrived. Alonzo, now fifty years old and Annie, forty-seven, brought this "late-life child" into the world in 1900. Leah was a cherished and much loved little girl at the Dos Rios. Aunt Susan, her nurse, watched over her every move. Her parents, older siblings, and two grandmothers, doted on her. As a little girl she had great collections of dolls and was a dog fancier with a large assortment of dog photographs, dog statues, and of course, the dogs themselves who were allowed to stay in the house with her. Beloved Leah would prove to be a bonus child, a blessing and a bastion of love and support for Alonzo and Annie for the rest of their lives.

In addition to the extended Hartman family, many guests were welcomed at the castle over the years. It was a very "social place" – perhaps one of Gunnison's foremost. The Hartmans enjoyed entertaining and there were occasions when more than a hundred guests were invited for some special event. Among these were Annie's regular "Monday Afternoon Club" members, local matrons who would be entertained and then served elegant lunches. On Sundays school friends were invited over for taffy pulls. Bruce and Hazel gave parties in the hayloft of the barn –

hay racks picked up the guests. A "Grandma Party" was held in 1900 attended by 20 grandmothers representing 90 grandchildren. Alonzo and Annie celebrated their 25th wedding anniversary in the castle in January of 1907. A dance was held and twenty-five guests were served cake that had been decorated in silver and white and garnished with wedding rings. All these various events were special ones in Gunnison and were regularly reported in the local newspapers.

Perhaps the most impressive celebration held at the castle was Hazel Hartman's wedding in 1910. The ceremony took place in the library of the castle. The local newspapers reported "the bride was attired in a beautiful gown of white marquisette over cream white satin, trimmed with pearl beads, silver lace, and a bit of old lace. Hazel came down the stairway and entered the library on the arm of her father. The bride and groom were married under an arch of white and yellow chrysanthemums by the big bay window." Writing of this event in his memoirs, Alonzo reported; *"In 1910 Hazel was married to Ernest Kingbury of Booneville, Missouri, a fruit grower and merchant. She looked very beautiful in her wedding dress. How we hated to lose her."*

* * *

(Shortly after Hazel's wedding the halcyon days for the family at the Dos Rios came to an end with Alonzo's unexpected decision to sell the ranch. Alonzo's memoirs are unclear about whether the family moved out of the castle at the time of this sale or a few years later – but local newspapers report that the ranch itself was sold in 1911. At some point in time the family returned to the stone house in town that they still owned. From the 1911 sale of the ranch and on up until the present day, the Dos Rios has gone through a long succession of owners. Perhaps the Dos Rios' best days, after the Hartmans left it, were when it was purchased by prominent local rancher Craig Goodwin and his wife Kate. They bought the Dos Rios in 1942 and owned it until the early 60s. The Goodwins restored the, by then, rundown mansion to a semblance of its former "ranch house/castle" glory and maintained much of the original Dos Rios property as a ranch.

Since the time of the Goodman's "Gunnison Hereford Ranch" occupation, the castle has gone through various owners and through various phases of both loving care and tragic deterioration. But for a short time the castle was revived and turned into the elegant "Fisherman's Inn" restaurant. The castle's historic features were part of its Victorian décor.

Alonzo's Dos Rios Ranch in its prime had reached roughly from the confluence of the Tomichi and Gunnison rivers southwest of Gunnison to the foothills of the Hartman Rocks area and included the present-day Dos Rios subdivision and much of the hay meadow acreage located further to the west. A third or more of the former ranch has been subdivided but many of its original lush hay meadows remain and are in production with various adjoining ranches. At the writing of this book, current castle owner Dave Taylor is in the process of another renovation, hoping to preserve many of the historic features of the castle. And many of them remain, among them the beautiful ascending stained glass windows, several original fireplaces with the World's Fair Italian statues still in place, the ancient woodwork, the fancy filigree over doors, Annie's painting turret, and the beautiful oak staircase where now upon entering the old abandoned house one can almost see lovely Hazel Hartman descending the stairs on the arm of her father on her wedding day.

A FAMILY PHOTO ALBUM

Cameras became available to the general public in about 1900 and, fortunately for posterity, the Hartman family had one and someone – perhaps young Hazel Hartman – took priceless pictures. Other, more formal, portraits were also taken of some of the family members. Here are some of the family photos.

All photos from the Bruce Hartman photo collection
Courtesy of Duane Vandenbusche

A formal portrait taken the day before Alonzo and Annie Leah Haigler were married (January 29, 1882).

Thirteen grandmothers pictured at the
"Grandmother Party," 1900.

Annie and Leah, 1903.

Bruce, Hazel and Leah, 1903.

Leah and dolls, 1905.

Pals – Leah and favorite dog, 1905.

Bruce Hartman
as a young man
about 1910.

First day of school for Leah and cousin Emily in 1906.

Hazel in her
wedding dress,
1910.

Leah and cousin Emily in 1909.

Hartman family and friends in front of the Dos Rios
"Castle," 1908.

A young Bruce Hartman on "Outlaw" around 1900.

Leah and her nurse "Aunt Susan," 1903.

Leah, left, and Hazel at Dos Rios around 1920.

Annie and Alonzo in their later years.

Another great photo of Alonzo and Annie.

TWO NEW HOMES

Their first house in town on Wisconsin Street. Alonzo
and Annie lived here from about 1884 to 1886.

Walt Barron photo (2012)

The Hartman's frame house at Dos Rios.

Walt Barron photo (2012)

THE HARTMAN CASTLE

An early picture of the home long referred to as "The Hartman Castle" built at Dos Rios in 1891. (All the Hartman homes, built in the late 1880s - the frame house, the "Hartman Castle" at Dos Rios, and the stone house on Wisconsin Street - survive.)

Staircase and stained glass windows in the "Castle."
Walt Barron photo (2012)

Another view of the staircase and windows.
Walt Barron photo (2012)

The oak staircase from the ground floor.

Walt Barron photo (2012)

A downstairs fireplace.

Walt Barron photo (2012)

Part VII

The Last Round-Up

T he local folks in Gunnison, the friends and neighbors of Alonzo and Annie Hartman, must have been in for quite a shock upon reading the *Gunnison News Champion*, Oct 20, 1911. It stated: *"Probably the largest land deal ever consummated on the Western Slope was completed here Wednesday when Hartman Ranches were sold or rather exchanged toward 4,000 acres of land, water rights, reservoirs, etc., in West Paradox.* (In Montrose County) *Besides the 2200 acres owned by Hartman at Gunnison, his brothers F.J. (Joe) Hartman of Montrose goes into the deal with the Riverside Sanitarium and 22 acres near that city, while E.R. (Edward) Hartman of Maher puts in 500 acres. Associated with them will be B.W. Marsh, a well known promoter and ranchman of Montrose who has large holdings in Paradox, probably 6,000 acres in all."*

Hartman had been such a mainstay in the community for so long – nearly forty years - and had achieved such success as a cattleman, that his abrupt decision to sell the Dos Rios and relocate for a potentially risky proposition elsewhere was totally unexpected. Alonzo was sixty years old at this time, and claimed that advancing years and the fact that his only son, Bruce apparently had little interest in the ranch were in part responsible for his decision. But perhaps it is best to let Hartman speak for himself on this matter. From his memoirs: *"I had hoped that I could turn the ranch over to Bruce. But after he finished college, he married a girl from Utah and moved there to live. . . Leah decided that she wanted to be a teacher, and we decided to sell Dos Rios and move back to the stone house on Wisconsin. But my brothers Joe and Ed had become interested in the Paradox Valley in Montrose County where, they said, the land was so fertile that peaches grew as big as cantaloupes and pumpkins weighed twenty-five pounds. We thought if we all put our money together, we could build a dam and irrigate many small fruit and vegetable farms.* They (the brothers) *had heard from a party of Hungarians who would like to come to the United States only if they had a definite place to go. They were all skilled farmers and could pay for the land. But a strange thing happened. We had always let a party of gypsies camp on our land every spring as they came through Gunnison. An old gypsy woman came up to Annie and said, 'Your husband wants to sell your ranch and move to a far country. But don't let him do this to you. It will bring you nothing but unhappiness' ... It was only a coincidence that her prophecy came true. For after we got the dam and reservoir* (Buckeye Reservoir) *finished, the first world war broke out, and the Hungarians were not allowed to leave. No one else wanted small farms, so we all lost most of our money."*

There were a few details left out of Hartman's casual account of losing much of his fortune on this project. His new "Eldorado" was started in 1911 - Hartman, and two of his brothers risking nearly all they had on the venture. Together they formed the Paradox Valley Irrigation Land and Development Company and became the principal stockholders in it. Three years into the project, by 1916, the Hartman brothers had acquired much of the tillable acreage in the West Paradox Valley and things were looking good. Many laborers were hired and the project was progressing as planned. But by 1917, things changed and they found themselves in trouble. The advent of World War I had caused the cost of labor and materials to greatly increase and the project became much more expensive to continue with. Then a dam broke, washing out many of the would be farmers who had by this time come to the Paradox Valley hoping for the irrigation water to materialize so they could begin cultivating their new farms. Many of them now pulled up stakes and left. In 1920, the by then floundering company went into receivership. As Alonzo admitted in his memoirs . . . he and his brothers had lost most of their money. His resources greatly depleted, Alonzo came home.

Fortunately the Hartman family hadn't entirely left Gunnison when Dos Rio was sold. Information is very sketchy on this point but it is known that the first winter after the ranch was sold, Bruce and Alonzo went back and forth to Paradox tending the new project and Annie and Leah stayed in Gunnison. After that it appears that the family resided in both Paradox and the stone house in Gunnison – possibly going back and forth. It is unknown if or for how long the entire family lived in Paradox. In 1920, after the failure of the water project, Bruce left for what would be permanent residence in Utah.

All that is known of the Hartman family for the next few years, now composed of Alonzo, Annie, and Leah, is that they resided in Gunnison until about 1926. By then Leah had graduated from Gunnison's "Normal School" and completed her training to become a teacher. Alonzo's next mention of their circumstances in his memoirs is that when Leah got a teaching position in California, Alonzo and Annie moved out there to be with her. Thus Alonzo ened his more than fifty-year tenure as a foremost resident of the Gunnison Country. He was, in fact, a "father of the Gunnison Country."

Alonzo and Annie thenceforth visited or lived with one child or another after leaving Gunnison. They spent a year or so visiting Bruce in Utah. Bruce eventually became a very successful "fox farmer" there. They stayed with Hazel for a year in 1929, at her home in Missouri. Otherwise they lived out their remaining years in the home of Leah Cunius, their now married daughter, in California. They faithfully returned to Gunnison every summer though, until 1935, attending Cattlemen's Days, Pioneer Banquets and celebrations.

Alonzo spent much of his time in his golden years writing his memoirs and various other accounts of the early days in the Gunnison Country. About this new writing pursuit, he stated: *"There wasn't enough to do to keep me busy* (in California) *so I started writing these memories of my youth. Gunnison will always seem like home to Annie and me; for we had our happiest days there, but California climate is easier for our old bones."* Most of his writings and many family photographs were donated by his son Bruce to noted local historian Dr. Duane Vandenbusche. Other of the family's possessions were donated to Gunnison's Pioneer Museum and are on display there.

Alonzo and Annie celebrated their Golden Anniversary in Lynwood, California in 1932, with their daughter Leah and many friends and relatives. Alonzo died in 1940 at Leah's home in Mojave, California at the age of 89, following a stroke. Annie died at her daughter's home a few years later, having outlived Alonzo by several years. All of the couple's children lived long lives but none of them produced any children of their own, grandchildren for Annie and Alonzo Hartman. Therefore, sadly, no descendants exist.

It is hard, writing of Alonzo Hartman's life, not to idolize the man. In all that I read of him, I never saw any serious criticisms. Reading between the lines, about the only negative thing one could possibly say of him was that he, being a workaholic himself, could sometimes be a very hard task master with his hired help. I had to wonder if this included his son and if that was the reason Bruce walked away from the Hartman empire. However, I do not know this to be a fact. It also could be said that he seemingly did not flinch at, in all likelihood, taking a lead role in one of the brutal sheep killings in early-day Gunnison.

Other than that, I will let the man's sterling record speak for itself and conclude with the words of two friends who wrote of him at his death:

"His development of Dos Rios ranch is a fine demonstration of his aspirations . . . also he was a devoted husband and father, as evidenced by the respect and almost reverence of his wife and children for him."

"He was one of the real pioneers of Gunnison County. Friends will indeed miss this hardy pioneer, who was known to all for his honest and upright character, his sturdy and undaunted courage, and his industrious life."

The Hartman family in an undated photo. From left, unknown, Alonzo, Annie, Leah, Bruce, unknown, Hazel.

Dos Rios Memories

Epilogue

A portion of a popular recreation
area south of Gunnison officially
known as "Hartman Rocks"

What if it were somehow possible for the ghost of Alonzo Hartman to come back to the Gunnison Country for just a day and ride his horse through that wonderful country of his, that "new Eldorado" he discovered nearly a century and a half ago? What would he see and what would his thoughts be? Of course he would find the wild empty country he rode into on Christmas day in 1872 greatly changed, and yet much of what was once dear to him would remain and he would recognize it.

He would find all his former dwelling places still standing – all except the original cabins of the cow camp. His post office, greatly restored from when he last saw it crumbling away at the Dos Rios Ranch, he would now find standing strong and sturdy on the museum grounds east of town, facilities that did not even exist when he left the Gunnison Country. His stone house on Wisconsin Street would be seen as little changed. the old fashioned windows are still in place and the hop vines, possibly planted by Annie, are still growing up the sides of the house. He would find his "castle" at the Dos Rios much the worse for wear but still standing, greatly resembling its old self and in the process of being restored to its former glory. The carriage house behind the mansion would look almost the same as when Alonzo and Annie lived there. The sturdy brick barn, his pride and joy, and the sheds, corrals, and other outbuildings, so much a part of any ranch, are all gone now because sadly, the Dos Rios isn't a ranch anymore. His remote line camp cabin, located half-way between Gunnison and Taylor Park, would be found in ruins and barely upright in a lonesome gulch that hardly anyone ever visits and if they did, they would not know of its significance.

The town of Gunnison would be a marvel to him, sprawled out in all directions from where he originally helped plat it in the sagebrush. The town's former dirt streets, all that Alonzo ever knew during his tenure here, he would find still wide but now paved. Not to be seen by Alonzo would be the elegant La Veta Hotel where he and Annie led the Grand March so long ago, the building being entirely gone. Gunnison's "Normal College" where Leah attended when it was comprised of nothing but a building or two including Taylor Hall, would be seen by Alonzo today as the beautiful landscaped campus of Western State Colorado University, spread out over several blocks with many attractive buildings – old and new.

East of town Alonzo would find the country not greatly changed from what he once knew and with many families carrying the names of the grandfathers and great grandfathers who had pioneered with Alonzo when the country was new.

North of Gunnison Hartman would find the Ohio Creek Valley still incredibly beautiful but much developed from the sparsely located pastoral ranches of his time. The once familiar and thriving town of Baldwin he would see as a crumbling ghost town now, and the old Fairview School House, would be found deserted but still standing and the view is as fair as ever.

Traveling to the northeast, Alonzo would surely be surprised to find a sprawling mass of condos, houses and buildings consisting of the towns of Crested Butte, Mt. Crested Butte, and Crested Butte South. In Alonzo's time Crested Butte had been nothing more than a little mining town and in his memory the surrounding country was what was significant. To him it was part of a great "cattle country." It was near here that the East Side Cattle Pool had grazed their cattle in the summer months and where nearby an unlucky herder's band of sheep met their fate one day at the hands of cattlemen.

Perhaps the greatest change to be seen by Alonzo would be the area to the west where he, Kelly and Jocknick had long ago trailed Ute cattle over country heretofore only traversed by Indian trails. He would look with amazement upon Blue Mesa Reservoir, the largest body of water in Colorado, nearly twenty-six miles long and covering up the old town sites once familiar to him – Sapinero, Cebolla, Kezar, and Iola. Numerous ranches or ranch/resorts once known to Hartman would be covered by water, a thing he probably would have thought impossible.

Hartman's old cattle range in the Taylor Park area would offer another surprise to the old cowboy who had long trailed his cattle there. Hartman was gone from the Gunnison Country when Taylor Park Reservoir was completed in 1935 – about the time of Alonzo's last summer visit to the area. It is possible that he saw the project in some stage of construction but the finished product, a reservoir that flooded forever more than 2,000 acres of grass plains, would surely have astonished him.

If Alonzo's last stop on his visit was a return to his beloved Union Park, he probably would feel right at home. At last he could step back in time, truly come back, come home to a place so little changed from what he once knew. The ancient Union Park cow camp cabin, where he had stayed with the other old-time cowboys would be nearly the same as he had left it a century ago. And the park itself, would be still lovely with vast grasslands virtually unchanged and undeveloped. Here there would remain a bit of the last of the old West. It would be a welcome sight to the old cattleman, one perhaps summed up best by a stanza of Badger Clark's poem, *The Passing of the Trail*.

There was a sunny, savage land,

Beneath the eagle's wings,

And there across the thorns and sand,

Wild drovers rode as kings.

BIBLIOGRAPHY

BOOKS

Bowen, A.W. and Co., eds. *Progressive Men of Western Colorado.* Chicago: A.W. Bowen and Co., 1905.

Brown, Dee. *Bury My Heart at Wounded Knee – An Indian History of the American West.* New York, Chicago, and San Francisco: Holt, Rinehart & Winston, 1971.

Choate, Julian Ernest, Jr., and Frantz, Joe B. *The American Cowboy.* Norman: University of Oklahoma Press, 1955.

Dallas, Sandra. *Gas Lights and Gingerbread.* Denver: Sage Books, 1965.

Frink, Maurice. *When Grass Was King.* University of Colorado Press, 1956.

Goff, Richard, McCaffree, Robert, and Sterbenz, Doris. *Centennial Brand Book.* Colorado Cattlemen's Centennial Commission. Denver, Colorado. 1967.

Ingersall, Ernest. *Knocking Around the Rockies.* New York: Harper Brothers, 1883.

Jocknick, Sidney. *Early Days on the Western Slope of Colorado.* The Rio Grande Press, Inc., 1913.

Morgan, Robert. *Boone – A Biography.* Chapel Hill, North Carolina: Algonquin Books of Chapel Hill, 2008.

Osgood, Ernest. *The Day of the Cattleman.* University of Chicago Press, 1929.

Perry, Eleanor. *Colorado's Taylor Park Shangri-la*. Self published. USA. 1929.

Rockwell, Wilson. *Uncompahgre Country*. Lake City, Colorado: Western Reflections Publishing, 2000.

Sammons, Judy Buffington. *Keepin' the Peace – Early-day Justice on Colorado's Western Slope*. Lake City, Colorado: Western Reflections Publishing, 2010.

Sammons, Judy Buffington. *Tall Grass and Good Cattle – A Century of Ranching in the Gunnison Country*. Gunnison, Colorado: Western State College Foundation, 2003.

Sandoz, Mari. *The Cattlemen*. Lincoln and London: University of Colorado Press, 1958.

Smith, David and Becker, Cynthia. *Chipeta – Queen of the Utes*. Lake City, Colorado: Western Reflections Publishing, 2003.

Smith, David. *Ouray – Chief of the Utes*. Ridgway, Colorado: Wayfinder Press, 1987.

Tucker, E.F. *Otto Mears and the San Juans*. Lake City, Colorado: Western Reflections Publishing, 2003.

Vandenbusche, Duane. *The Gunnison Country*. B&B Printers, Gunnison, Inc., 1988.

Vandenbusche, Duane and Smith, Duane A. *A Land Alone: Colorado's Western Slope*. Boulder, Colorado: Pruett Publishing Company, 1981.

Wallace, Betty. *Gunnison Country*. Denver: Sage Books, 1960.

Wallace, Betty. *History with the Hide Off.* Denver: Sage Books, 1964.

PERIODICALS/THESES/REPORTS

Borland, Dr. Lois. "Ho for the Reservation." Undated manuscript, Gunnison County Library, Gunnison, Colorado.

Cummins, D.H. "Social and Economic History of Southwestern Colorado, 1860-1948." Ph.D. Thesis: University of Texas, 1951.

Easterly, Lewis H. "The Agricultural and Livestock Interest of Gunnison County." Gunnison, Colorado, 1916.

"Frontier in Transition: A History of Southwestern Colorado." Bureau of Land Management Cultural Resources Series: No. 10, Chapter IV.

Gunnison County Stockgrowers Association's Minute Books. 1894-1911. In possession of the Gunnison County Stockgrowers Association. Gunnison, Colorado.

Hartman, Alonzo. "Early Days in Gunnison, Colorado"-"My Life"-"When Whites Decided to Send Utes to Uncompahgre Reservation About 1872" – "August 1, 1872 With General Charles Adams and Otto Mears at Ute Reservation on Cochetopa" – "Boyhood Memories of Alonzo Hartman" – "Early Days in the Gunnison Country" – "Memories and Experiences With Ute Indians in Colorado." Dr. Duane Vandenbusche collection at Western State Colorado University.

Hoeppner, Richard. "Los Pinos: A Study in the Change of the Ute Indian Way of Life and Government." Unpublished Masters Thesis, Western State Colorado University, Gunnison, Colorado, 1973.

Jackson, William Henry. "A Visit to the Los Pinos Agency in 1874." *The Colorado Magazine,* Volume XV, 1938.

Kerr, Bill. "Gunnison National Forest: A Brief History." Undated document. USFS files. Gunnison, Colorado office.

Kitson, Ray. "Crooksville." Unpublished Thesis, Western State Colorado University, History Department, Gunnison, Colorado. 1983.

Landwehr, Marcia Wright. "Ranching on the Cochetopa." Unpublished Thesis, Western State Colorado University Library, Ranching Heritage Project, Helen Jensen Western History Room.

Lloyd, John B., "The Uncompahgre Utes." Unpublished Masters Thesis, Western State Colorado University, Gunnison, Colorado, 1932.

Reppy, Mamie McConnell. "The McConnell Clan." Duane Vandenbusche collection. Western State Colorado University, Gunnison, Colorado.

Sammons, Judy Buffington, *Gunnison County Stockgrowers 1894-1994 – Anniversary Issue.* Gunnison, B&B Printers, 1994.

Sammons, Judy Buffington, "Not All Lost at Los Pinos." *The Gunnison Country Magazine,* 2008.

Sammons, William Perry, Diary – 1928. Author's collection.

Taylor, Kent. "The House That Hartman Built." Unpublished Thesis, Western State Colorado University, Gunnison, Colorado.

Wallace, Betty. "Six Beans in the Wheel." Unpublished MastersThesis, Western State Colorado University, Gunnison, Colorado. May, 1956.

NEWSPAPERS

Gunnison Tribune, 1891-1900.

Gunnison News Champion, December 29, 1922, July 18, 1935, February 15, 22,26,29, and March 7, 1940, December 17, 1942, November 17, 1960, April 7, 1966.

INTERVIEWS

Marcia Wright Landwehr with:

   Parker McDonough, February, 1981, Gunnison, Colorado

Personal interviews with:

   Joyce Hartman, Montrose, Colorado, December 2012

   Gib Kysar, October, 2012, Taylor Park, Gunnison, CO

   Marie McDonough Sammons, July, 1996, Gunnison, CO

   Paul Vader, September, 1996, Vader Cloverleaf Ranch, Gunnison, CO

ABOUT THE AUTHOR

Judy Buffington Sammons grew up on a Hereford ranch in the beautiful Ohio Creek Valley just northwest of Gunnison. She holds a Master of Arts degree in Education from Western State Colorado University and has recently retired from a 30-year career teaching math, reading, and English in the field of Adult Education. She enjoys hiking, reading, spending time with family and grandchildren and pursuing her retirement calling and great love which is writing. She is the author of six books and numerous articles on western Colorado history. She is a member of Western Writers of America.

Log on to <u>www.raspberrycreekbooks.com</u>
to order this book and others from the publisher.
They are also available in bookstores, on Amazon.com,
and also via Barnes and Noble and Ingram Book Company.

CPSIA information can be obtained
at www.ICGtesting.com
Printed in the USA
FSOW01n1553281114
3620FS

9 780985 135225